Black Males IN THE Green Mountains

Rochelle Brock and Richard Greggory Johnson III
Executive Editors

Vol. 38

The Black Studies and Critical Thinking series
is part of the Peter Lang Education list.
Every volume is peer reviewed and meets
the highest quality standards for content and production.

PETER LANG
New York • Washington, D.C./Baltimore • Bern
Frankfurt • Berlin • Brussels • Vienna • Oxford

DENISE HELEN DUNBAR

Black Males IN THE Green Mountains

Colorblindness and Cultural Competence in Vermont Public Schools

PETER LANG
New York • Washington, D.C./Baltimore • Bern
Frankfurt • Berlin • Brussels • Vienna • Oxford

Library of Congress Cataloging-in-Publication Data
Dunbar, Denise Helen.
Black males in the Green Mountains: colorblindness and cultural
competence in Vermont public schools / Denise Helen Dunbar.
p. cm. — (Black studies and critical thinking; v. 38)
Includes bibliographical references and index.
1. African American young men—Education—Vermont—History.
2. Public schools—Vermont—History. 3. Education—Vermont—History.
4. Discrimination in education—Vermont. 5. Racism—Vermont.
6. Vermont—Race relations. I. Title.
LC2731.D86   371.829'9607309743—dc23   2012007135
ISBN 978-1-4331-1762-6 (hardcover)
ISBN 978-1-4331-1761-9 (paperback)
ISBN 978-1-4539-0806-8 (e-book)
ISSN 1947-5985

Bibliographic information published by **Die Deutsche Nationalbibliothek**.
Die Deutsche Nationalbibliothek lists this publication in the "Deutsche
Nationalbibliografie"; detailed bibliographic data is available
on the Internet at http://dnb.d-nb.de/.

The paper in this book meets the guidelines for permanence and durability
of the Committee on Production Guidelines for Book Longevity
of the Council of Library Resources.

© 2013 Peter Lang Publishing, Inc., New York
29 Broadway, 18th floor, New York, NY 10006
www.peterlang.com

Printed in the United States of America

FOR

MY

GABRIEL

ACKNOWLEDGMENTS

The journey to completing this book has been by no means a solo endeavor, but a shared process. Many family and friends have shown their generosity by supporting me in countless ways. First and foremost I honor my ancestors whose shoulders I stand on: my grandmothers, daughters of the African Diaspora, and my grandfathers, too. To my loving parents, Kenneth and Evelyn Dunbar, both of who put education high on their list of hopes and aspirations for their progeny. Even though I took many detours to get here I cannot thank them enough for never giving up on me.

Dr. Richard Greggory Johnson III, you have been a well of inspiration throughout this whole process. Thank you, Dr. Robert Nash, Dr. Binta M. Colley, and Dr. Stephanie Seguino. To all of you I am deeply grateful. Thank you to my many professors, whose encouraging words and actions were always in support of my social justice work, especially Dr. Judith Aiken and Dr. David Shiman. Dr. Sue Fleming, thank you for sparking and encouraging my passion for educational justice through the frame of critical race theory.

Also, thank you to my first academic/social justice inspirations at the State University of New York College at Old Westbury, the first multicultural college in the SUNY system: Professors Dr. Charshee L. McIntyre, and Dr. Council Taylor. Deep gratitude to my high school history teacher, Mrs. Carter, who kindled in me a deep love of African and African American history in 1968 at Roosevelt High School.

To my husband, Michael Thomas Heath, heartfelt thanks for humoring me when I needed it most and tending to the dinner on nights I was swamped with trying to complete this work. To my beautiful children, Kali and Ben Alvarez, Manus Dunbar Loecher, and Emily Heath, thank you for keeping it real and in perspective. To my grandson, Gabriel, "in all of my deliberations I think of you and those who will follow after you." My dear twin and hero, Darrell A. Dunbar, and my brother Kenneth S. Dunbar, I love you both. Carolyne Alicea, you are the epitome of a true best friend.

Thank you to my friend and travel buddy, Kim McRae. That journey to the Pacific was both rejuvenating and memorable. Shout out with much love and respect to anti-racist education activists, Paij Wadley-Bailey, Sha'an Mouliert, Aiyana Blackhawk, Pat Shine, Sara Martinez de Osaba, Corali Cotrina, Mercedes Mack, Lindsay Reid, and Jeanine Bunzigiye.

To Lola, my loyal study buddy, many thanks for making sure I didn't do all of this work in isolation. As usual, you stayed the course as only a faithful canine companion would.

To the team at Peter Lang, thank you for your patience and support in bringing this book to a tangible artifact. Sarah Stack my production coordinator, Phyllis Korber copyediting, Michael McFadden in marketing, thank you, thank you. Drs. Brock and Johnson, editors of the Black Studies and Critical Thinking series at Peter Lang, thanks for having faith in my work.

I want to offer posthumous thanks to Vermont's race women and men, who have been called home after opening the way to racial justice as well as offering their shoulders for us stand on. Lucy Terry Prince, Daisy Turner, Otis McRae, Larry McCrorey and John Tucker and numerous others.

I want to conclude by thanking as well as dedicating this work to my eldest brother and inspiration, John Leslie Howe Sr. I love you, bro, may you rest in power, 1947–2005.

In memory of Anthony Hunter Dandridge, 1990–2008

TABLE OF CONTENTS

Don't Believe the Hype

Being progressive, however, does not mean being anti-racist. (Al-Faruk, 1997, p. 12 as quoted in Vermont Advisory Committee to the United States Commission on Civil Rights, 1999, p. 18)

When the average person conjures up a vision of Vermont, many are likely to think of fall foliage, winter sports and progressive politics. Perhaps some may even recall Burlington's distinction as the birthplace of John Dewey, one of progressive education's most highly respected philosophers.[1] Or the green mountain states national reputation as being at the forefront of healthcare reform.[2] There is so much good intention, embossed in Vermont's cultural and social narrative, that anyone seeking a change from the hectic buzz of an intolerant life would be shortsighted not to take the chance to experience all of its dazzling attributes of acceptance and open-mindedness.

I often wonder what really attracted me to this beautiful state in the first place. I clearly recall my main impetus to relocate here, which stemmed from the drive to find a community of kindred spirits who practiced outside of mainstream dogma. Secondly, I was looking for a place with reputable colleges to consider when thinking about an advanced degree. Most importantly, however, I wanted to give my seven-year-old daughter the opportunity to experience a simple, safe lifestyle. In hindsight it was an easy decision.

Following the call to join with both nature and progressive thinkers in a somewhat provincial setting, free from the burdens of an existence influenced by urban decay, we both embarked on our journey. Deep down inside I secretly hoped that she would develop an appreciation for the simple abundance the environment had to offer, providing her with the gift of being connected to the land. An appreciation and love, which I developed and embraced during childhood visits to our family land, in the Blue Ridge Mountains of Virginia. Without an iota of doubt and led by my inner nomad, I immediately responded to the call. Taking heed with the best of intentions, I journeyed "up north" just after completing my undergraduate studies. To be honest, I was beguiled by the scenic splendor and beauty of the green mountains that seduced me from the very beginning.

Like many who have followed the drinking gourd before me, traveling north in search of new experiences, escaping the limitations of raising children in deteriorating school systems or in neighborhoods on the fringe of suburban decline, I too, set my sights on New England's Green Mountain state. Mainly because I believed it offered the simplicity my heart was in search of. All the enticing allures of a glossy ad to a Shangri-la type destination, lay before me. Pointing the way for a new and liberating lifestyle. Just like numerous similar-minded folk, over the years, driven by a desire to settle and raise families in this naturally beautiful, rural, northern state, which, at least by all accounts, initially appeared to me to be safe and inclusive. Why wouldn't one be enamored with the enticing advertising of what seemed on the surface a racially accepting paradise?

Over a short period of time, however, the utopian mystique that held me captive wore off, opening my eyes, revealing the state's pretty checkered history, in terms of race relations. After many personal hits and misses across the racial divide, I learned rather quickly that there actually exists a uniquely troublesome history, a seamier side of the green mountain state. At first it was hard to believe that Vermont, quite vocal in its antislavery rhetoric, is known as having a documented history of racial, as well as religious intolerance, bigotry, and hatred. With the passing of time I learned, not to believe all of the hype. Especially when it came to the dealings of the institutions and school systems and the social interactions with residents who identify as people of color.

Furthermore, the most apparent warnings to catch my attention and concern, however, were some troublesome incidents occurring in a variety of classrooms across the state. The most disconcerting in nature were the allegations that some students of color and their families were not being treated with the respect and care they deserved in the public schools (Vermont Advisory Committee to the United States Commission on Civil Rights, 1999).

Microaggressions (Sue, et al., 2007) and stereotype threats (Steele & Aronson, 1995) seemed to be the context in which race based bullying and harassment were played out. According to psychologist Wing Sue, microaggressions are "brief and at times commonplace daily verbal, behavioral, or environmental indignities, whether intentional or unintentional, that communicate hostile, derogatory, or negative racial slights and insults toward people of color, in which the perpetrator is most likely unconsciously unaware" (p. 271). Micro aggressions appear in three forms as: microassault, microinsult and microinvalidation and can be more commonplace in which almost all interracial encounters are prone (p. 271). The uniqueness of this liberal phenomenon however, is its everyday occurrence, making it the new face of everyday racism in the post civil rights era (p. 272). In my view microaggressions are the underbelly of bullying and harassment that is both race based and overlooked in our schools and are presented not only as student on student but adult-to-adult and adult to student as well.

Stereotype threat, a term coined by psychologists Claude Steele and Joshua Aronson (1995), however, is "being at risk of confirming, as self-characteristic, a negative stereotype about one's own group" (p. 797). And its prevalence in our society raises possibility for potential targets that the threat stereotype is true of them and also for people who see them that way. For example, a student of color has anxiety around self-fulfilling the racial stereotype of their groups intellectual capabilities as being less than those in the dominant group. Nonetheless, the damaging impact of negative stereotypes as well as assaults on ones own reality due to group membership over time has affects on both the social and emotional well-being (Sue et al., 2007, p. 272), safety, as well as academic achievement for many students of color (Steele & Aronson, 1995, p. 798). If students of color have anxiety over perceived deficiencies' assigned to their racial and ethnic group and it is articulated through direct and indirect messages, anxiety, as well as the possibility of fulfilling the prophecy is likely to occur. Modern racism perpetrated through both micro aggression and through stereotype threat creates an underlying tone in the schools social climate that has a toll on students as well as adults of color sense of safety and well-being.

Hence, when the news broke in 1997 about institutional and individual acts of racial injustice, I was not too surprised when allegations of racism in Vermont public schools surfaced. In hindsight, I could not help consider my own life where I've had to deal with similar incidents, which in my perceptions were racial in nature, yet tended to like they were inconsequential or just in my imaginings. I clearly remember one incident in particular, when one of my children had to deal with a swastika etched on a computer disk, to then have the incident minimized and dismissed as " boys will be boys" by a school administrator when I brought it to the schools attention. An assortment of race based microassaults and stereotype threats on my students' humanity, as well as dismissive attitudes on the part of school leadership over the course of time made me realize that Vermont was not the race neutral zone it had stubbornly proclaimed to be. Don't get me wrong, because in most of my dealings with school and my children, I have had the pleasure of also dealing across the racial divide with teachers and administrators who were aware, culturally competent, very supportive and caring as well.

Nevertheless, after much deliberation over the newfound facts related to hostile school climates and students of color, my concern became a deeper cause for advocacy and justice through the power of presence in teaching and learning. Naturally, the educator/activist in me, immediately reached out across the divide and made myself available to the school community by going into classrooms too share my story as a person who has witnessed and experienced injustice based on race, class, ethnicity and gender, up close. I strongly believed then as I do now, that by being available to dialog with students about my life and personal experiences during Jim Crow and the early civil rights era, would help students gain an understanding as well as appreciation from a first person perspective. I felt it would be a way to provide them with perspectives outside of the norms with which they may or may not have been familiar.

Moreover, I believe the more students have the opportunity to interface with people who identify differently from the norm, the more they have an opportunity to learn from others through their individual experiences. All too often we learn about others, not as individuals, but as members of a specific social group. This, in my perspective, is very dangerous. Dangerous in that no one can lay claim to being the voice for an entire group. I only speak from my own personal experiences, as a parent and former student who has had to negotiate a system that on occasion was not very welcoming and at times wrought with unintended bias. Nevertheless, I have always endeavored to place my voice and perspectives at the table for justice and equity when advocating on behalf of myself, and my children.

One voice, however, that is apparently missing from the social discourse in the area of Vermont public schooling, is the collective voice of what is in many ways is a growing demographic: student voice and students of color voice in particular. If our states public schools are not prepared on the most basic level to provide a safe and inclusive environment for students of color, as well as others marginalized by social identity, they create a missed opportunity to be at the forefront of education equity for all of Vermont students.

From my perspective as social observer, and in all of my deliberations as an education activist, I continually ask myself, what has demographic growth meant for students, particularly African American or Black males (henceforth Black males)[3] attending public schools in the predominantly White, rural communities of Vermont? How do school climate, discipline practice, teacher attitudes and perceptions, access to enrichment affect them? What are their final outcomes as far as college and preparation for life after secondary school? I wondered just how well Vermont's males of color were doing, considering the state of educational equity and achievement on the national level for both Black and Latino males.

Furthermore over the years, the green mountains have attracted an abundance of new citizens from a variety of racial, ethnic, and linguistic backgrounds in search of the same quality of life in the states neighborhoods and communities that is both safe and welcoming. Vermont's newest residents are rapidly changing the cultural, ethnic, and racial landscape of communities as well as schools that have been traditionally White (United States Census Bureau, 2010).

For instance, in one of the state's largest and most diverse school districts, 27% of the students identify as students of color (Burlington School District, Annual Report, 2011). This is rather remarkable for many reasons. First, the state is following a national trend, which reveal population shifts in small towns and rural areas that have included people of color, immigrants, and refugees to the growth. Secondly, empirical studies over the past twenty years have looked at student graduation rates, achievement, and aspiration, particularly among students of color and Black males in general, by focusing on urban areas where critical mass in populations of color resides. Very little inquiry, however, has been undertaken in the rural areas of the nations northeastern regions that have been predominantly White, but, are undergoing rapidly shifting racial and ethnic demographics, quite similar to what is happening right here in Vermont. With schools being the first to reflect population shifts in a community, I often wonder how prepared the public schools are in meeting the needs of a vastly diverse student body that identify outside the norm, especially students who identify as African American/Black? Are they prepared and aware of the impacts that demographic racial shifts create? What does the research tell us about the phenomenon?

One such study in a liberal Midwestern town (Kailin, 1999) intrigued me, and revealed some insightful data, related to perception and reality on educators attitudes towards race in a predominantly White, suburban community. "The study sought to understand how teachers perceptions of racism and race in their schools, impacted their role in transformational decision-making, in terms of both interpreting and responding to racial inequity." (724) Apart from Kailin's timely study, very little has been added to the growing body of research on the schooling experiences of Black males or students of color in areas that are traditionally White and rural, such as Vermont. The challenge for a state like Vermont, has been its lack of thoughtful and intentional preparedness in addressing the issues of growth that have resulted in frictions, tensions and misunderstandings in both the schools and in the community at large among different community members.

Furthermore, for a state like Vermont, there has been minimal, if any, information on students of color and their public schooling experiences from the primary or first person perspective. The data that we do have access to reveal standardized test scores and graduation rates by race, inclusive of both genders.[4] It's not clearly apparent, however, just how well Black males are doing as a discrete population. Very little statewide data exists to date that address aspiration, achievement, and attainment for Black males. The educational community does however, have access to race/gender-disaggregated data, based on access to enrichment, student discipline and suspensions as well as special education, but there is a limited amount (if any) of data on race or gender (as a separate disaggregate) available on graduation and dropout rates. Aside from some public investigations into allegations of race-based bullying and harassment in some school districts across the state (Vermont Advisory Committee, 1999, 2003), no data on schooling experiences based on students' voices and perceptions are available to date. Hence, the lack of data by local districts prohibits the public from having access to useful information, which may prove helpful in providing best practice based on an inclusive, multicultural framework and a culturally responsive pedagogy when serving not only students of color which in the long run also is positive for their White counterparts as well.

With the state's rapid growth in multicultural and ethnic diversity and its history of racial bullying and harassment in the public schools as well as throughout the state in general, comes with it a reasonable amount of tension and missteps around seeing and serving new populations equitably and fairly. Community-wide tensions and perspectives around available resources, differences in viewpoint, as well as turf, are what fuels distrust in the institution is to be expected. Nowhere are these collisions of both social and cultural norms more evident and likely to first emerge than in situations where structural inequity and hegemonic power traditionally prevail such as within the school (Spring, 2008).

What are Vermont schools and communities doing to provide equitable educational outcomes for all students, especially students of color? Is Vermont prepared for the new majority at the dawn of this new millennium?

Twenty-First-Century Schools, Twentieth-Century Consciousness

At the turn of the last century, educator and statistician Leonard Ayres asserted, "no standard which may be applied to a school system as a measure of accomplishment is more significant than that which tells us what proportion of the pupils who enter the first grade succeed in reaching the final grade" (Ayres, 1909, p. 8, as quoted in Weis & Fine, 2005, p. 21). The emphasis on the student reaching the final destination via the monitoring of graduation rates, then later dropout rates has been the central focus in monitoring outcomes for public school students.

Furthermore, education reform efforts within the past thirty years have myopically focused on the destination, with minimal consideration given to the experiences of the student, between entry and departure. The measure of graduation rates at the close of the twentieth century has been one of the greatest indicators of how well both schools and students are doing in terms of moving towards that goal (Weis & Fine, 2005, p. 21). However, Ayres's supposition was valuable in terms of White students, but it was myopic in the context of the present-day schooling experiences as well as achievement outcomes for students marginalized by race.

Nonetheless, Ayres may have overlooked as well as failed to recognize the social and cultural structures within the school, which prove prohibitive for marginalized populations from actually arriving at that final destination with not only the diploma but, also with their dignity, self-esteem and humanity intact. Graduation rates may give us some of the picture, but do not give us the full picture. Other indicators such as college attainment and the acquisition of skills necessary for meaningful life work also have significant value in gauging success. Most importantly in the era of safe and inclusive schools however, both academic and the social experiences of the student also hold tremendous capital and are likely to determine a student's aspiration and level of academic achievement as well.

Over the past decade, underachievement and high dropout rates amongst urban Black and Latino males have raised widespread concern across the nation due to the phenomenon's disproportionate nature.[5] For a population that comprises only 12.4% of the national total, 50% of Black males do not finish high school.[6] In 2007 the overall national graduation rate was 69%. The nation's lowest performing high schools produced 58% of all African American dropouts and 50% of all Hispanic dropouts, compared to 22% of all White dropouts.[7] Furthermore national numbers inform us that African American males are the most at risk for failing and dropping out of school because of their disproportionate representation in special education classes, low ability tracking, and suspensions, harsh discipline practices, the negative effects of zero tolerance policy, as well as the low expectations from their teachers.[8]

Theorists analyzing the public school experiences of Black males have provided a variety of explanations for this phenomenon. Research has investigated the ways in which Black males are alienated in environments that impact their safety as well as interrupt aspiration and achievement. The hypotheses range from blaming the victim and their families, cultural based incongruence's based on race to deficiencies on the part of the institution (MacLeod, 1987; Noguera, 2008; Ogbu, 1978, 1987).

What are the factors that have led to such disproportionate outcomes? What do the statistics say about places that are neither urban nor suburban, but rural instead? Places that are traditionally White and unmistakably rural like Vermont, the second Whitest state in the union.

I firmly believe that Black male students' overrepresentation in these types of doomful scenarios is not the result of innate deficiencies in intellect or culture, as claimed by some of the research that has sought to analyze the reasons for school failure. Rather, the system in and of itself is inherently flawed. Flawed by injustices based in history (Spring, 2010), internalized bias, color blindness,[9] stereotypical thinking, teacher relationship dynamics,[10] low expectations, and levels of cultural incompetence on part of both the institutional and individual level.[11]

From where I stand, Black students are not the ones underachieving; it may just be the school system that is. The achievement gap phenomenon is not just the province of poverty, as some are quick to claim, because in reality, it is happening to a large proportion of Black males regardless of parental socioeconomic status (Allen, 2010). Despite their middle-class status, young Black men are not exempt from racial microaggressions and stereotype threats (p. 127). Social experiences that lead to unsafe school climate, which in turn affects achievement.

The public school experiences of some Black males, regardless of their socioeconomic status, have not been much different from those of their peers in other parts of the nation. According to a recent report on African American males, published by Schott Foundation on Education (an national education advocacy organization), shows statistics which indicate that Black males are graduating in Vermont, to the point of an inverted gap.[12] However, the report goes on to say that African American males are overrepresented in special education, are disproportionately suspended, and are underrepresented in academic enrichment classes in the schools. This data is a quandary to me because it exposes what seems to be a dichotomous phenomenon: graduation rates that are awesome yet glaring in disproportional disparities.

What the research has not explored, as is the case in Vermont, is what young men of color are experiencing inside the schools in terms of climate, discipline practice, teacher relationships, and expectations for their success by those charged with guiding them inside the school to graduation. Yes, parents and guardians are extremely important to the success of the student, however, the adults inside the building are equally important, too. In my mind the support for success is a two-way street. These factors are all too important to both meaningful experiences and successful school outcomes. We have a lot of literature that speaks to and has measured this phenomenon. One critical measure that is missing however, that may help us get to the bottom of what is really going on for students of color is their personal viewpoint about their schooling experiences.

This text strives to bring to light the perspectives of thirteen Black males who had attended public schools in a variety of locations throughout the state. A variety of young men, who have willingly revisited the past by opening their hearts, in order to share their stories as well as insights. Their unacknowledged narratives speak to the individual and collective journeys they have traveled in order to reach the final destination of graduation.

Let us now bare witness as former public school students talk about resilience, resistance, as well as transformation in the face of the "best of intentions." Moreover, their subjugated stories counter the stock stories (Bell, 2010) that are so much a part of living as a person marginalized by race in not only America, but in Vermont as well.

I believe that only their personal journey through school from their own standpoints can help those who will follow in their footsteps. By sharing histories, they will hopefully become affirmed as well as validated through the sheer act of personal disclosure. The individual and collective perspectives may well represent the voice of many Black males waiting to be heard and acknowledged here in the shadows of the green mountains.

Concealed Voices Countering
the Stock Stories of Hegemony

When I started elementary school, there was a lot of, I wouldn't say so much overt racists or racism, but there was a lot of irrelevant name-calling such as the word 'nigger'; so I got suspended a lot for fighting with people calling me 'nigger.' (Field notes)

The above quote is a preview of the concealed voice of the new face of Vermont. This entry is a snippet of a narrative that speaks to the story-teller's experience as a Black male, a student of the new millennium, recounting his schooling from his own reality. Silenced perspectives that have been subjugated, for too long.

Why storytelling (Bell, 2010) or in this case what I would call per-spective? First, I believe that disclosure from the first person standpoint is the most powerful way to gain understanding into an individual lived experience. Especially information that seems hard to retrieve in the form of statistical data. For me as a social justice advocate, sharing experience as a mode of inquiry provides a framework for me to gain an understanding that validates the individual experience of the partici-pant. Secondly and most importantly, they who feel it know it.

Perhaps, it is because I feel that the lack of primary information available about Vermont's males of color is a form of marginality in and of itself and shows on a certain level, a lack of visibility, forethought and caring. Collecting the shared wisdom that collective experience bestow, has helped me to develop a more critical understanding of how race and racism operate both culturally and institutionally in the school setting. The urgency for me though, or at least the red flags, is the early indica-tors outlined in state and federal reports many years ago. These trends for Vermont's Black males have been following those at the national level in both suspensions and special education usage. I couldn't under-stand the lack of urgency on the part of those in positions of leadership. I wondered who was actually awake and connecting the dots. From the early indications via community as well as data, I recognized the ur-gency, and thus deemed it important that we seek the perspectives of former students themselves. In addition, I realized that the subjugated view might just prove to be useful in providing a powerful backdrop for cross-racial understanding as well as provide the opportunity and space for social equity and action within the school (Bell, 2010, p. 16) as well.

Through the exploration of all of the stories available in Vermont, especially the master narrative via stock stories, I have come to a deeper understanding of the tales Whites folks tell themselves and each other consciously and unconsciously, in order to keep hegemony in place, right here in liberal Vermont.

Some White people, as well as some people of color, are deeply invested in these master narratives, which can be defined as "a set of typical, all too familiar stories held in reserve to explain racial dynamics in ways that support social position in the racial and social class hierarchy" (p. 29). We are all too familiar with these kinds of stories. Stories that explain away injustice such as for example, the "myth of meritocracy," or "the bootstrap theory" which explains away institutional inequity or "Black families don't value education," to the destructive myth of "Black criminality"—all stories that many of us have been socialized to believe about others, who are racially and ethnically different.

Furthermore, what is being concealed if we do not consider the perspectives of those who are impacted by the dictates of power? The power to not even consider marginalized experiences, when they are occurring in clear sight is evident to me. I understand that institutions are fearful of seeking what they may consider anecdotal information as data. However, there is nothing more liberating than revealing the subjugated standpoint that has been suppressed and concealed through the power of personal voice. Concealed stories (Delgado, 1995) are the hidden omissions, which coexist alongside the dominant storyline. Counter-storytelling on the other hand challenges the traditional mythology of hegemony by telling the story from the reality of the "other" (Delgado, 1995, p. xiv)—and in the case of students of color in Vermont, the reality of dreams deferred, threats because of entrenched stereotypes, racial micro aggressions in daily experiences, as well as diminished access to the rewards of equitable public education. Hence the experiences I describe and analyze here are the insights of former Vermont public school students who identify as both Black and male.

Throughout Vermont, the prevailing stock stories however, are informed by liberal notions of a slave-free republic; inclusive and safe schools for students of color; and Ruby Payne (2001) with her troubling, flawed analysis of poverty and race.[13] In her book, *A Framework for*

Understanding Poverty, Payne speaks as an "expert" on the mind-sets that drive class position and status. Her unscholarly work is packed with "undercover" stock stories, which, left to the uncritical mind, contributes to the perpetuation of myths about people in poverty as well as people of color. She renders race invisible by making it clear upfront, that her framework is not about race, yet negative racial stereotypes are clearly apparent and abundantly present throughout the text (Gorski, 2008). With pathological preciseness she erroneously points out in her case studies, criminal or violent behavior as a natural aspect of the "other." The characters illustrated in her case studies are symbolically portrayed as, predominantly people of color. Starting with the notion that people in poverty possess deviant behaviors—like knowing how to get out of jail—is pretty racist, in my mind. Not once did she talk about the community networks, created by people experiencing economic challenges, which are models for building strong community, such as sharing resources as well as property.[14] Cultural ways of being that reside outside of the traditionally held notion of "rugged individualism."

Moreover, Payne, a self proclaimed title as a class "expert," talked about the mind-set of poverty and the hidden rules of class without addressing the capitalist system in which poverty found its genesis and the racism and classism engendered as a means to perpetuate class and race divisions and social inequity. Nevertheless, Payne's work I think, is nothing more than a conservative, classist strategy, employed to unconsciously disparage marginalized groups, while holding them accountable to the hegemonic norms that prevent them from succeeding in our schools and society in the first place. Hence, Vermont cannot claim to be culturally competent in institutional practices if overlooking identity and defining people with stereotypes and assumptions taught through Payne's framework in the human service community. In sum Ruby Payne and cultural competence do not belong in the same venue when striving for social justice.

If we are going to investigate poverty without taking a deeper look at the root causes of poverty—hence, inequity in all its intersections—then we are wasting the taxpayers' dollars by blindly colluding in both racism and classism in our human service agencies, nonprofits, and schools. The elements of Payne's programming are tools to further unwittingly, confuse and confound those with good intentions, unconsciously leading them to unknowingly divide and oppress folks on the margins. In order to make systemic change we must start with ourselves as humans who bring all of our beliefs and biases into our practice—even those of which we may not be proud.

It may be somewhat true that liberal, progressive Vermont may have made a non-thinking decision that is currently causing more unintended consequences and damage than good in our institutions. Seeking to understand poverty through a framework that has no scientific grounding is in hindsight not culturally sensitive to marginalized communities and populations experiencing economic challenges. As educators and leaders we must remember one of the most fundamental practices in our field: reflection. Hence, by not reflecting on the dominant stories we were socialized to believe about difference (especially poverty), and without investigating our own social lens, we will not be as effective as leaders in making school an inclusive, rigorous and safe place where all students flourish. We can only achieve that by listening to what Black males and other students of color themselves have to say, about school. For their stories are filled with evidence as well as wisdom and insight. We must also be prepared for them to tell us things about race, class, and other difference that we may not be willing to hear. Nonetheless, we must be fully present with our ears and hearts open to what they have to say and suggest, regardless of how fearful we adults may be.

I have often found it unsettling that I can go into classrooms today with a racial justice literacy program that I coordinate, engaging the race discussion with children and a few community members committed to racial justice, yet have resistance from those unable to see the social factors that contribute to inequity such as race and class. However, when it comes to a civil community-wide discourse about race and racism in the schools, all opportunity to get to the work of social justice is stifled. The disease of colorblindness, cloaked in fear, and denial are at the core of the problem. If we can let go of our defenses we may just make gains in becoming equitable in both policy and practice.

Based on conversations, young Black men talk about the old and new form of institutionalized racism: color blindness, in their schooling experiences. The aftereffects and consequences range from social isolation to bullying and harassment, school discipline practice, special education, as well as the curriculum and teachers' expectations. Their views bring to light incidents of micro aggressions,[15] as well as stereotype threats,[16] all of which not only deeply impact a students humanity but also affect the ability to learn in a safe, hostile-free environment. They all speak about the positive influences that a few teachers have had on them as well. It is their wisdom that is at the center of this text. Once we take to heart and consider the perspectives of our students, we as educators and leaders can develop new insights into what really contributes to a safe environment that directly contributes to equitable achievement outcomes for students of color in rural, traditionally White spheres. My hope is that this endeavor will do just that, so all students will reach and achieve their highest potential especially students of color and others traditionally marginalized.

Minority underachievement and high dropout rates have been at the center of school reform discourse. Quantitative research has provided statistical data on this issue. Very little if any quantitative statistics on school performance in Vermont, however, is disaggregated by race and gender (Vermont Department of Education, 2010) as well as a system that makes capturing the data efficacious. With that in mind I became curious as to the experiences of students of color in Vermont public schools.

Moreover, it is important to understand, that not all the experiences of males marginalized by race or social class are the same, and just as clearly, this text is by no means trying to weed out "racists." However, the research does inform us that there is a distinct connection between race and gender as it applies to disparities in discipline policy and practice (Ferguson, 2001; Reyes, 2006), placement in special education (Kunjufu, 2005), as well as teacher attitudes and expectations (Delpit, 1995; Gay, 2010; Hallinan, 2008; Monroe, 2005). These all have some bearing on the success and achievement of Black students—especially males. All too often, though, their experiences are formed by a majority of incidents in the school climate, from stereotype threats and micro aggressions, to the long held flawed belief in black criminality, bullying and harassment, unjust discipline practices, and low teacher expectations.

In Vermont, we do not really know how well African American males are doing as a discrete population. Very little data address aspiration, achievement, and attainment for the high school population. However, the educational community has access to disaggregated data based on student suspensions and special education, but there is no data on race or gender (as separate disaggregates) available on graduation and dropout rates. The public does not know how well this particular population of students is faring in our public schools because we have no actual data to assess them. We cannot say that Vermont is any different from the rest of the nation due to those factors. Furthermore, theorists have come to a variety of conclusions about Black males and their schooling experiences.

Vermont the second Whitest state in the United States (US Census, 2010), and is by no means, free of a history of racial bigotry in the community and in the schools (Vermont Advisory Committee to the United States Commission on Civil Rights, 1999). Observations over time and responses to allegations of racism tell us so. The genesis of racism in Vermont lies in the displacement and deculturalization of the Dawnland or Wabanaki people to recent allegations of racism in the public schools. Hence, I am of the belief that allegations of racial harassment have elements of microaggressions stereotype threat, color blindness, and a lack of cultural competence as factors in equitable social and emotional outcomes.

Without having any disaggregated data available that break down achievement, and because it has been difficult to examine the facts of what is actually happening in Vermont public schools for Black males, my journey endeavored to expose the issues at the very core and bring to light what may actually be happening. In all of my efforts to obtain Vermont-centric information (without much success), I decided to find out on my own by asking Black males directly what their public school experiences were like. For along time I've been deeply interested in their perspective, as should all of us who are committed to dismantling inequity in our institutions and because America's history is a history of racism and intolerance. Public school is the place where most social and racial inequities play out (Anyon, 1981; Bourdieu, 1977; Spring, 2008). In order to dismantle racial injustice and inequity, an understanding of the history of institutional racism and its impact on the humanity, and academic success of students of color must not be overlooked, but be made central to both teacher training and professional development of twenty-first-century educators. Teachers who's' classrooms will present a variety of social and cultural identities.

Across the nation much has been done in an attempt to create safe, caring, meaningful, and equitable school environments on behalf of students of color especially males. I ask then: why do we still have such high rates of underachievement and lack of attainment attributed to them? Maybe we have been looking in the wrong spheres and asking the wrong questions?

I believe we can find out directly from former students themselves. It is their message, via their personal narrative, that drives my purpose to deliver their hidden voice in the shadows of the Green Mountains to an audience unaware of them and their educational circumstance. Some members of the community have been slow to respond to their concerns. Whatever the reason for this disregard may be, those in charge need to hear loud and clear that some Black males, even though they may be high school graduates, are disappointed in a system filled with missed opportunity and broken promises. If Black men feel let down then we, as educators have not been wise in our care for all students in this beautiful state. We must all see this issues as our issue not just the issue of individuals affected. "What the best and wisest parent wants for his own child, that must the community want for all of its children. Any other ideal for our schools is narrow and unlovely; acted upon, it destroys our democracy" (Dewey, 1959, p. 34). If we are to actualize the dream of democracy here in the green mountains, then we must be willing to see that all of our children are deserving of an equitable education, not just a privileged few.

Furthermore, we must not fool ourselves with the denial attributed to color blindness because there is a well-documented history of race-based bullying and harassment in Vermont public schools going back fifteen years (Vermont Advisory Committee to the United States Commission on Civil Rights, 1999, 2003). The most complicated issue outlined in the reporting was the denial of some in positions of leadership about these issues. I believe that both color blindness, lack of urgency and an unwillingness to do anything about it played a big factor.

Moreover, bullying and harassment of both racial and ethnic minority students in the state has seen an unfortunate revival recently. As recently as 2009, out of the 2,465 youths surveyed who identified as racial and ethnic minorities, 11% skipped school due to feeling unsafe en route to or at school (compared to 5% of their White counterparts); 14% were threatened or injured with weapons at school (compared to 5% of their White counterparts); 24% were bullied (compared to 15% of their White counterparts); 40% experienced physical fighting (compared to 26% of their White counterparts); and 11% attempted suicide (compared to 4% of their White counterparts) (YRBS, Vermont Department of Health, 2009). We should be asking why are these numbers are up? They may just be a red flag telling us that something is not quite right in our public schools.

Much of the research on African American males and their public schooling that has analyzed achievement and success paints a bleak picture for a population that is overrepresented in special education classes, in the justice system, and in high dropout ratios. Students of color and especially males are suspended at disproportionately higher rates than their White counterparts. This phenomenon is a common occurrence. Indeed, cutting edge research informs us that no matter where Black males live or what their parents' socioeconomic status; they are not immune to the effects of White supremacy (Allen, 2010; Ogbu, 1987, 1992). Poverty alone does not explain the differences, because poor White males do just as well as African American boys who do not live in poverty, which is normally measured by whether they qualify for free and reduced lunches. We must look beyond the standard social factors, such as poverty, earlier considered important in researching the achievement gaps for students of color (Gabriel, 2010).

The problem, I feel, along with other activists, lies in the cultural divide so evident in our schools. It's the messages that are being sent to Black youth and how their peers, as well the adults in the building, relate to them too. The messages are based in both history and culture (Delpit, 1995; Gay, 2010; Ladson-Billings & Tate, 1995). I also clearly understand that this message is also directed at Black girls as well. However, in schools that stockpile Black boys in special education classes, track them to low-level courses, zealously enforce zero tolerance policy and harsh discipline practices, and hold low expectations, the message is clearly sent that black people are stupid criminals and unworthy of the opportunities to make a meaningful life for themselves through their education. These are the consequences of institutionalized racism, inequity, and injustice.

Please keep in mind this is not a tale of gloom and doom. Instead, it is a vehicle for the community writ large to finally hear what Black males who have attended Vermont's public schools have to say in their own voice. Their stories are an opportunity to speak their truth to power and make meaning out of their own schooling while opening the door to transformative action for those who will follow in their footsteps. Finally this is a wake-up call to consciousness, proclaiming that the promise of access to equal opportunity as a democratic principle is not equally obtainable for some of our citizens. The participants' accounts will remind us that, although there have been a few inroads made in transforming schools to meet the needs of all students, not much has changed since both state and federal investigations uncovered racial bullying and harassment close to fifteen years ago (Vermont Advisory Committee to the United States Commission on Civil Rights, 1999, 2003). We must remember that the allegation that many adults important to the conversation were not at the table (p. iii) because it appeared not to be urgent or important to even as populations continued to grow right before their eyes.

From what the participants have shared, I can only infer that the situation has remained relatively the same, with the possible exception that there may now be new populations of color who may also be affected. I often am concerned with a state like Vermont, which has not reconciled its racial past yet stands on its laurel of anti-slavery, will have these issues come back with some rude awakenings down the road. We have had many warnings and wake-up calls, but it seems as though folks are just comfortable staring at the elephant in the middle of the room waiting to be addressed. What will it take if we are not continuing the conversation? Refusal to deal with the issue of race, and just look through the lens of class has created a stubborn type of color blindness that may be impeding the progress of equity.

Personally, I am sick and tired of people telling me, "It's not about race it's about class," while all the coded talk as explained by Payne's text, it is about the intersection of both race and class. As an advocate for educational equity, I will not give up the cause for racial justice in our schools by being quiet. My moral conscience will not let me. Refusing to see the elephant in the middle of the room will by no means, make it disappear. Therefore, I want to bring that elephant back to the forefront of this conversation with a brief history of how students of color across the state have experienced their public schooling.

Vermont and Race Relations

Education, like "race," is situated in a context. There should be no need to go into great detail about the history of the education of Africans under slavery, coloniza-tion, apartheid, and white supremacy ideology. The record is clear. The treatment of Africans was not a matter of negligence or accident. It was not benign. Massive and strategic attempts were made to use educational structures to destroy "criti-cal consciousness," to alienate Africans from tradition and from each other, to teach African inferiority and European superiority. (Hilliard, 1998)

We do not have to inhabit environments that are heterogeneous by race to experience racism. As a matter of fact it can happen anywhere. Race issues are a part of the nations as well as the state's history because racial incidents occurred right here in the public schools not too long ago. During 1997, there were investigations into whether students were treated differently based on their race, and whether differing degrees of discipline were applied to minority students in the public schools throughout the state (Vermont Advisory Committee to the United States Commission on Civil Rights, 1999, p. iii). The response from the US Department of Educations Office of Civil Rights (OCR) to the issues occurring in Vermont schools was timely. Their investigations were prompted by the concerns of community members as well as by the parents of students who were "victimized by a hostile climate in their respective schools" (Vermont Advisory Committee to the United States Commission on Civil Rights, 1999, p. 2).

The Vermont Advisory Committee to the United States Commission on Civil Rights investigated minority student and their families' concerns on a variety of issues that were hindering students from feeling safe at both school or at school-related events (p. iii).

Over a period of two days, 36 community panelists offered rather candid views on racial harassment in the public schools. Eighteen parents and two students testified to a multitude of complaints ranging from outright physical abuse to cases of school staff and administrators not responding in a timely and just manner to end bullying and harassment that was racial in nature. The report noted, "The absence of important key figures in the educational community confirmed the lack of interest in the problem, believing that it was a general indifference to the problem of racial harassment" (p. iii). However, what was of greater importance was that the families of minority students had five issues that were of great concern relating to the educational experiences of their children: first was, a lack of respect and empathy shown by teachers and administrators towards minority student concerns; second, the use of curriculum materials promoting racial stereotypes; third, a presumption that minority students are involved in criminal activity; fourth, an unsatisfactory, school-based response to racial harassment incidents; and fifth, an overall climate of racism that exists throughout the state (p. 6).

The Commission's findings culminated in a 1999 report entitled "Racial Harassment in Vermont Public Schools," which provided highlights and testimony of the several issues that were of dire concern, to minority students and their families. There appeared to have been an overall lack of respect for students of color, especially related to teachers' and administrators' resistance to responding to racial issues. The disbelief by those in power, held capital because some felt that issues concerning students of color were anything but racial. Most were deeply vested in their own color blindness and unconscious internalized bias. In addition, among other concerns was the use of educational curricula that did not reflect the experiences of African American students that was stereotypical in nature. There also appeared to be an "overall climate of institutional racism that seemed to persist in Vermont public schools" (p. 6).

As a result of this report, it was determined that racial harassment was frequent across all grade levels, and that school personnel were ill equipped to respond appropriately to the incidences (p. 6). These experiences appeared to be linked to an underlying atmosphere of institutional racism and color blindness that is deeply prevalent in pubic school systems (Atwater, 2008). It was believed that elimination of these barriers was not a major priority among school administrators, school boards, elected officials, and some state agencies charged with civil rights enforcement (p. iii). Nonetheless, the Commission's report became a baseline reference as well as tangible evidence that racial issues were problematic in Vermont public schools. A follow-up report in 2003 basically made it very clear that racial intolerance was still endemic in the schools (Vermont Advisory Committee to the United States Commission on Civil Rights, 2003, p. 2).

Here we are in 2012, fifteen years after these investigations, and what has been done to change the situation? What we do know today is that conditions for students marginalized by race, class, ethnicity, and sexual orientation have gotten worse in this beautiful state (Vermont Department of Health, YRBS, 2009). Vermont should see this as a wake-up call and act before it is too late. It is not as if a history of discrimination towards non-Whites hasn't existed here, because the history speaks to a formidable presence called the KKK at the turn of the last century. [17]

What has been and still is the greatest stereotype threat to Black male students at the time is the falsely held belief in their assumed criminality as expressed in the report in (Vermont Advisory Committee to the United States Commission on Civil Rights, 1999, p. iii).

Research clearly tells us that school climate affects the achievement and attainment potential of students of color. Most importantly however, are the emotional costs of racism on not only students of color, but also on their White peers as well (Derman-Sparks & Ramsey, 2006).

An Urgent Call to Consciousness

If we are not paying attention by not making achievement data readily available, do we really know how well Black males are actually doing? We do know however, that they are disproportionally placed in special education, harshly disciplined and have little to no access to enrichment. I ask then how can they be reaching their highest potential if we have no measure on aspiration and attainment? If they are graduating, how well are they doing post school?

In my deliberations as an antiracist education activist, it has been a moral dilemma to remain silent on an issue that has been unanswered for too long. Moreover, whenever I bring up the questions about achievement, as a single disaggregate by both race and gender; I often encounter some defensive responses as well as harsh criticism. I have been labeled a troublemaker for asking questions that relate to the issues of equity as well. If we are to make any headway on the issue of achievement disaggregated by race and gender, then we must look at

ourselves as educational leaders and ask "How am I a part of the problem? Is my inaction and lack of urgency at the bottom of this problem,
too? What attitudes and beliefs do I hold that are part of the problem? Is
there anyone else who is as concerned as I?" Because I believe the right
to question is part of being a citizen in a democracy. Especially if inequity and injustice is staring you right in the face. I have always believed
that education is a human right.[18]

Since 2003, there seems to be an evasive attitude or what some may
refer to as a denial about discussing anything related to race and its
relationship to education equity and social justice. Even so, no quantifiable measure exists on the graduation or dropout rates as they apply to
Vermont's Black male students. There should be a sense of urgency in
wanting to know the facts. Wouldn't you want to know? Especially since
our schools are more diverse than ever before, and the forecasts say
growth will continue to increase.

In Burlington's public schools alone, there are more than fifty-seven
native languages spoken ("Burlington School District," 2011). Other
areas across the state, including rural areas, are experiencing demographic shifts as well. Hence, I think it would behoove both state and
local districts to have data on marginalized populations such as Black
males and other males of color who, according to the national numbers,
are not completing their education at the same level as their White
counterparts. And if they are, are they prepared for life post high school?
I believe that these are realistic questions to ask as we work towards
equity.

Moreover, in 2009, I had a conversation with the education commis-
sioner as to why we do not have these data at hand. As of 9/13/2010,
the calculation overview for graduation and dropout data on the Vermont Department of Education's (VT DOE) own website stated: "Until
Vermont has a more sophisticated student information system that
allows the drop out problem to be more accurately tracked at the
student level, this estimated rate is the best approximation currently
available. Because the rate is based on aggregate data (data of a population as a whole) it cannot be disaggregated, or broken up, by gender,
poverty or disability status. Nonetheless many educators are confident
that male students who live in poverty or who have disabilities account

for the large portion of students who drop out" (Vermont Department of Education, 2009).

When I look closely at the VT DOE disclaimer on its website, I can clearly see the invisibility of race/gender. The invisibility is evidence of the unimportance of Black males as a stand-alone disaggregates in calculating graduation and dropout rates. Moreover, how can the state overlook the factor of race when Vermont's public schools have had a long and emotional history with racism? Is it denial or color blindness or both, that is in the way?

I believe it is this lack of urgency around all things racial in the current school climate that has caught my attention. If we are to move forward in our mission to dismantle inequity and make schools socially just, we need to gain a broader understanding of the historical under-pinnings that play out in the school so that we may fully understand the conditions that Black males and other males of color may experience.

In a study on community factors that impact minority students' performance in the public school systems, Ogbu (1992), an educational anthropologist, focused his research on the experiences of voluntary and involuntary minorities in public school environments. His investigations have tried to find answers to the questions of why some minority groups are more successful in schools than others. The difference, he asserted, has to do with a variety of cultural and social factors. These factors are based on the shared, collective, historical experiences of voluntary and involuntary minority groups with dominant groups and the institutions they control.

Voluntary minorities such as ethnic Europeans, Asians, people of Caribbean descent, and Africans do not have the historical baggage that Black Americans have. Yet some may experience marginality in their lives. This statement is not meant to say that they do not experience the micro aggressions and stereotype threats that people of color and other subordinated groups' experience. However, involuntary minorities such as African Americans have historically been forced to maintain a subor-dinate status within American society through policy and practice that uphold second-class status in terms of education, housing, and health-care. The history of socially constructed myths about race and Blacks' presumed inferiority has also fed the collective consciousness that perpetuates those structures through a deficit lens.

Working in a variety of school districts across the state, I have personally witnessed attitudes and behaviors of a few school personnel that come from preconceived notions about people of color and those in poverty that are based in deficit thinking, color blindness and cultural incompetence. Being a witness to the types of bias that exist in institutions, I have had firsthand experience in dealing with misguided thinking that sometimes is present in collegial circles where such narrow thinking may present itself.

I could perhaps take up a whole chapter just in discussing situations where I feel a biased view was informed by deficit thinking. Instead I will share and deconstruct with you one incident.

Example 1: Deficit Thinking on the Part of Some Teachers.

This educator's perception of the student portrayed in the example was clear that although the student was not perceived as a criminal he was certainly seen as inferior in intellect. Cultural deficit theories perpetuate a detrimental cycle in our nation's education system, which holds groups marginalized by race and low income, students, and their families primarily accountable for their economic circumstance when various social factors may also play into the equation.

One personal example of the pervasiveness of deficit thinking that clearly stands out for me was an incident that occurred a few years ago while I was visiting a public school. An African American youth I knew appeared in an office, where I happened to be during my visit. Seeing this young person as he dropped off an assignment to his teacher in a public space was a highlight of my day. I greeted him and asked him how he was doing. After a brief conversation, he left and went about his business. A colleague in the office asked me how I knew the student. I responded that I had known him and his family for quite some time. My colleague quickly responded with a typical stereotype threat, "Well, you know he's a nice kid, but he's not the sharpest tool in the shed." This person did not realize that he had made an unwarranted, deficit-based, stereotypical comment in this very public space. I was totally put off because, even though I explained my relationship with this student and his family, the labeler felt privileged enough to put down this young man regardless of my affiliation to him. Did he expect me to agree with him? Not likely.

My response to his biased commentary was as follows: "I am surprised by your depiction of this young man, but most importantly, do you know who he really is?" I went on to state that he was a well-respected and loved member in his family and community. He was a hard worker and was respected for his perseverance, self-efficacy, and advocacy. In my eyes and the eyes of his community and family, he was an inspiration because of his strength of character and a role model for the younger members of the community.

This interaction with White teachers who manifest deficit thinking is exemplary of some that I have personally encountered with my colleagues. This situation, although disturbing, was very revealing as well. Nevertheless, this exchange was a perfect example of the deficit thinking, color blindness, and cultural incompetence that is all too often the operating norm in our schools today.

This portrayal of marginalized students within an education system set up to benefit and serve the best interests of the dominant society is not only unethical but also immoral and socially unjust (Spring, 2008; Tatum, 2008). At the core of deficit thinking is White privilege (McIntosh, 2000), as well as color blindness or denial in seeing the race-based injustices it perpetuates. This view of perceiving and defining non-Whites through the lens of White privilege and deficit thinking perpetuates outdated social notions and assumptions about race, thus inhibiting the progress so needed in our schools. Self-reflection is a key attribute in examining how we as educators participate consciously or unconsciously in racial inequity. We must develop a critical self-reflective lens in order to make change. We must engage ourselves in seeing our students in all of their identities.

Critical race theory in education according to an essay by Hall and Parker (2007), "Rethinking No Child Left-Behind Using critical race theory," portrays American racism as a persistent, historical and ideological construct that accounts for inequities such as dropout rates and school suspension rates for Blacks, Latinos, American Indians, and Asian Americans/Pacific Islanders (p. 135).

Vaught and Castagno (2008) examined what teachers' attitudes reveal about the structural dimensions of racial inequity in the schooling and achievement of underserved students. The researchers argued that "[the] thematically grouped racial attitudes of white privilege, individualism, and cultural awareness expressed by teachers are illustrative of larger structural racism that informs and is reinforced by teachers' attitudes as well as its' [sic] manifestation in practice" (p. 95). Attitude and awareness as well as self-analysis are essential in becoming an anti-racist educator dedicated to dismantling social injustice and racial inequities.

I know that if I am silent on an issue that is national in proportion, then, in reality, I am colluding with the structures and powers that I am committed to dismantling. I could not live with a clear conscience knowing that there is a history of inequity in Vermont public schools and that I did nothing to help to transform that inequity into justice. The central issues to conversations on transforming schools must no longer remain invisible. Race, class, and language must be visible to the process. I must, however, send a strong message that we are not as prepared for the growing diverse populations in our school system as we may think we are. The warnings in the form of rapid demographic shift and the report on racial bullying and harassment in Vermont public schools was tossed to the wayside. Today we are seeing the lack of taking the recommendations put forth in the Advisory Committee's report play out today as the landscape is becoming more diverse and visible.

According to the 2010 US Census, Vermont was the second Whitest state in the country, with Maine taking first place (United States Census Bureau, 2010). Vermont's total population is 625,741 (United States Census Bureau, 2010). Of that total population, 596,292 identify as White, translating into approximately 95.3% of the total population. Of the non-White populations here, 6,277 residents identify as African American/Black. Although African American/Blacks make up 1% of the total state population; this total represents a 37.2% increase in the entire population growth of African Americans since the last decade (United States Census Bureau, 2010). What is critical, however, is that the Chittenden County area alone is home to almost half of the state's total population of African Americans (3,319), with Burlington being a major place of residence. These data indicate a significant growth over a short span of time. Along with this rapid growth of racial and ethnic diversity have come both gifts and challenges in terms of intolerance, racial bias, and bigotry in many public sectors such as business, schools, and the judicial system. Furthermore, these data are essential to providing an education that is both excellent and equitable for all students. In order to level the playing field, schools need to be committed to the success of all students.

While engaged in trying to find educational data for Vermont, I located a report by the Schott Foundation informally entitled the "Black Boys Report" (Schott Foundation for Public Education, 2010). In this state-by-state report, the statistics provided quantitative measures on the achievement gaps of Black males in the nation's public schools.

According to the state breakout, the report's findings on Vermont. The data suggest that the state provides opportunities for Black students to learn that are equal to that of their, White counterparts in the public schools. According to the report, there are no inequities in education for Black males in Vermont public schools. Moreover, the report states that there is an inverted gap of -6% (Schott Foundation for Public Education, 2010). What I find intriguing about this breakout report is that there are numbers claiming to be representative of the Vermont's African American or Black male student population in the public schools. However, as stated earlier, it had been made clear that the state has no system in place that combines both race and gender as a single disaggregate (i.e., Black males). Thus, the question remains, how did the Schott Foundation get its data? Upon a closer investigation, there are no representative numbers by race as the report breaks down the state comparison to national numbers. What is even more intriguing is that further data cited from the Office of Civil Rights (OCR) showed huge disparities in special education, suspensions, and gifted and talented placement in comparison to White males as well. What is Vermont doing that there should be such great disparities in suspensions, special education, and gifted and talented placement, yet students are graduating to a point of an inverted gap? How are schools overcoming these claimed disparities among graduating students? Are they just pushing students through the system?

The report goes further to state, that half as many suspensions as a percentage of school population were given to Black, male, non-Latino students than to White, male, non-Latino students in Vermont in the 2006–2007 school year, according to the Office of Civil Rights of the US Department of Education (Schott Foundation for Public Education, 2010). Almost twice as many White male students as Black male students in proportion to enrollment were allowed to take advanced placement mathematics, and three times as many White male students as Black male students in proportion to enrollment were allowed to take advanced placement science classes in Vermont. These contradictions are what have me deeply curious, enough to ask what is going on.

The primary goal of this work is to bring to light the everyday schooling experiences of Black males from their own perspectives, in order to gain deeper insight into how school served their educational aspirations. The persons sharing are young men who've attended public school here in Vermont. Another goal is to influence education policy and practices that have direct bearing on how Black and other males of color are educated. Black males' schooling experiences and the history of racial inequity in Vermont's public schools are at the center of this story.

The premise is to keep the history of inequity and the public schooling experiences of people of color in Vermont visible and on the table for discussion as we make plans for the decades ahead. My hope is that race and class will not be factors in access, inclusion and equity for all students. Because there exists however, qualitative evidence of racism in Vermont and its public schools, this work seeks to countervail the pathology and deficit lens applied to the education of students of color in general, but especially males. This text examines their schooling through the theoretical lens of critical race theory.

The most significant reasoning behind this journey to follow my curiosity is due to the lack of urgency on the part of some districts across the state in providing disaggregated data on Black males in the public schools and the ability for the public to have access to it Another benefit of having such a timely study is that it will provide a baseline of information, encompassing the lived schooling experiences of some of Vermont's males of color. Research on this phenomenon in Vermont is virtually nonexistent.

Because of my interest in utilizing personal narrative and storytelling as a means to reclaiming subjugated voices as a tool for racial and social justice, I embarked on this project willing to speak directly with the young men who were on the front lines in schools on a daily basis. Because of my need to know and the need of this underserved community to be heard, this study addresses an urgent and timely issue. As a result of my passion for justice, I embarked on this journey to not only find answers but to discover the perspective of those whose voice has been hidden for too long.

The young men with whom I spoke on this journey had much to say about their experiences in Vermont's public schools. They candidly shared their stories of what it means to be Black and male in predominantly White schools in townships, hamlets and rural communities throughout the state. Their stories speak to resiliency, resistance, personal responsibility, as well as redemption. In the next chapter I will lay out what the body of literature says about critical race theory in the context of public schooling and Black males.

In the meantime as minority populations are predicted to grow rapidly, bringing more diversity to the state, it is imperative that we gain an understanding of what it means to be a student of color in predominantly White schools with predominantly White teachers. I am also curious how Black students from other countries perceive their own schooling experiences in communities and public schools that are predominantly White? How do they perceive their experiences in terms of discipline, climate, peer and teacher relationships, as well as social systems of support within the school? How did they experience support in meeting their goals to succeed and aspire? These are the questions we need to ask as our communities become more and more colorful and ethnically diverse.

Conclusion: My Personal Is My Political

As a woman of color living in Vermont with my own trajectory around racial marginalization here in the green mountain state, I am concerned for all students regardless of their identities, who have to contend with the complexities of racism in the world and particularly in the school setting. In recent years schools have been declared safe zones. Unfortunately students experience the contradictions of racial inequality in a society that prides itself on being a pluralistically inclusive democracy; creating a dissonance that only dual messaging creates. Messages conscious and unconscious, directed to all students, which in the end inhibits their social and emotional development. White children are stifled by the racist society that they grow up in, socially disabling them when working across cultural difference and in building authentic relationships between themselves and others.

My children and I have experienced numerous incidences of overt racism here in Vermont, which have occurred in both the workplace and in schools. I've been told directly on a few occasions, that I was a good little "nigger." Some readers may say that the transgressor was simply ignorant, attributing these encounters to bad behavior or to the individuals' attitudes. And that I should just close my eyes to it and ignore it. No matter how noble that position may sound, I don't buy into the maxim of "sticks and stones will break my bones and names will never hurt me." I find it a cop out to try and minimize another's experience with micro aggressions and stereotype threats. It's damaging regardless. Furthermore, if people right here in Vermont (who may not have had much interaction with racial diversity) are behaving this way in offices and schools, could it be that what they learned in school and the greater society reinforced their assumptions about the world and culturally dominated groups like African Americans and other non-Whites? Could old social events sanctioned by the local university, such as the "Kake Walk," have influenced their perceptions? The Kake Walk was an event that the whole community embraced as a family fun event. The fun in the form of racial satire was a means of subliminally and overtly endowing many of the states' citizens with a national, racist ideology through explicit use of stereotypical racist imagery.

Being a child of the Jim Crow 1950s, my educational trajectory reminds me of how far the school system still have to go in order to serve its marginalized citizens justly. I was a cultural outsider growing up in school, yet a triangulated insider to the goings-on in my own brothers' classrooms. Some of those experiences were very difficult for me personally. My early experiences in school were often very painful due to preconceived notions held by teachers, yet I managed to overcome the lack of care and the prevalence of racism and found hope through the support of my extended family and a few caring teachers. Sometimes I wonder how I was able to come to the other side unscathed.

In *A Life in School: What the Teacher Learned*, Jane Tompkins's narrative spoke to her experiences with the profession of teaching and the process of childrearing (Tompkins, 1996). She spoke out about the oppression or "child abuse" that some students suffer at the hands of family members (Tompkins, 1996, p. 6). I feel that teachers in many ways function as our surrogate parents while we are away from home, and that students also can experience abuse at the hands of their teachers. Tompkins quoted what Alice Miller (1990) labeled a pedagogy that produces oppression, which starts early and comes from traditions of childrearing such as those Alice Miller described in *For Your Own Good: Hidden Cruelty in Child-Rearing and the Roots of Violence*. "Childrearing is basically directed not towards the child's welfare but toward satisfying the parents' need for power or revenge." This need is created by abuse suffered and forgotten. "It is precisely those events that have never been come to terms with that must seek an outlet." Furthermore, Miller pointed out that "The jubilation characteristic of those who declare war is the expression of the revived hope of finally being able to avenge earlier debasement and presumably also of relief at finally being permitted to hate and shout" (Miller, 1990, as quoted in Tompkins, 1996, p. 6).

The majority of us have at one time or another during childhood been victims of the "pedagogy of oppression." Unfortunately, being oppressed as a child is often an inescapable aspect at the very center of the human condition. The adults in our lives—especially our schoolteachers—were our "surrogate" parents, to whom we were entrusted by our families from early morning until late afternoon. Indeed, as in my experience, no matter how hard I tried to be the good student, retribution sought me out, taking me by surprise when I least expected it. The hate and vengeful wrath targeted me straight in my developing sense of self, at times knocking the wind out of my homegrown confidence. You see, my first teachers were surrogate mothers. I sometimes think that my first five years in school made me somewhat the neurotic person I am today. Many of my fears, such as heights, and basements, maybe even rejection, have taken years of soul-searching and reflection to overcome. At school, fear came in the form of corporal punishment. The school climate there was a haven for fear and abuse, both physically and emotionally.

I did not know what a "spanking" machine was until I heard teachers threaten to send students across a bridge to the principal's office if they did not comply with the strict rules and constraints imposed upon them. The "spanking machine," which supposedly existed in a room in the dark, dank recesses of the basement of this gray and dismal building coerced me into becoming somewhat compliant and excessively nervous. At times I was so overcome by fear, it was not uncommon for me to pee my pants at the thought of impending punishment in the form of a teacher. The sight of her meant that someone was going to have to negotiate the larger-than-life bridge to get to the basement where the mysterious room that housed the machine of doom existed. This initially awe-inspiring building became an esteem-deflating institution of fear and aggression.

Being the attentive student that I aspired to be, I became compliant and constantly fearful of teacher retribution. I managed to do well academically until the fourth grade when I found myself a scapegoat for my brothers' teacher. I learned early on that if teachers did not like a family member, they probably would not like any others in the family no matter how "good" one tried to be. This one particular teacher was a notorious bully and would on occasion actually request that I come out of my classroom where she would embarrassingly shout at me, while poking her finger in my chest, electing me the "go between." I was the one assigned to carry her messages home to my parents about my brothers' assumed misbehaviors. We were told on numerous occasions that our family should pack our bags and go back to Africa. Being a second-generation Caribbean American and a descendent of exploited captive Africans, that incident became a game changer for my mother.

The conundrum for me about my own schooling was that it was constantly drilled into our heads that we were all "God's children." Even so, the hateful behavior imposed on me by this teacher, made me question whether I was little more than God's stepchild. I cannot imagine how my brothers, who were bright boys, fared through such blatantly intimidating acts of individual and institutional bigotry. Like many Black children, I grew up knowing racism existed because those experiences were the grounds on which we as a family discussed the good and not so good that existed in the world. Am I clouded or jaded by my experience? I think I have developed an ability to have compassion for folks who have not been able to see that race is still a very salient aspect of American society. Not talking about the ramifications of racial injustice will not make it disappear. Its manifestations have far greater consequences by not having the "talk."

Perhaps, my bias could cloud this analysis. I am not only concerned for students of color but for all students. I believe, however, that my lens can work for the greater good because of not only my shared status in terms of marginality by race and social class, but also because of my sensitivity to the issues that are faced by minority students is astute. Apparently, my background and experiences as well as passion for justice, have motivated me to co-create positive change in the lives of all students through the social justice work in which I engage in the classroom and community. Furthermore, I also am fully cognizant that I live in a state that has had a checkered past, including the presence of the Ku Klux Klan [19] at the turn of the last century, racial apartheid research at the University of Vermont (known as the "Eugenics" program)[20] and recent allegations of institutional racism in its public schools. This history is what has moved me to action. Therefore, I feel it would be unjust and unethical to the educational future of all male students of color in the state not to respond by asking them directly what their reality was in their public schooling.

What deeply moves me to take urgent and immediate action on behalf of Black males and their schooling however, is the disproportionate number of Black men in our jails, not only in Vermont but also across the country. We all know on some level that this situation is immoral and unconscionable. Here in Vermont, Black men are disproportionately incarcerated in comparison to their White peers (Greene, Pranis, & Ziedenberg, 2006). The reports and research tell us so. Thus, in my position of leadership and in my spheres of influence, I must also be diligent in building bridges of understanding across race, class, and gender. To do so would help in interrupting hegemonic practices that stifle and prohibit positive outcomes for the Black males in our community.

Those of us, who are genuinely invested in the well-being and potential of all of Vermont's students, need to be open to hearing and seeing what has been invisible and silenced for too long: the color blindness that further perpetuates inequity and cultural incompetence in our schools. What these young Black men have to say is crucial in shaping policy that will affect future students of color, who will be in attendance in our schools.

In Chapter Two, "Does Race Still Matter?" I will discuss race as a socio-historical construction, and present the literature on Black males and public schooling through the conceptual framework of critical race theory.

In Chapter Three, "In the Field," I will introduce the reader to my field experience, describing the task of finding participants and detailing how I engaged them in their perspectives.

In Chapter Four, "Voices From the Field," I introduce the reader to the participants' perspectives in response to the twelve interview questions I put before them. I compare them to the national stories of the experiences of others, the effects of discipline practice and suspensions, the overrepresentation of African American males in special education, and the impact of teacher expectation on achievement and success.

I conclude with Chapter Five, "From Color Blindness to Color Talk." In this closing chapter, I discuss the importance of lifting the veil of colorblindness in order to be an effective leader, as well as an effective antiracist, culturally responsive pedagogic practitioner. I also address the imperative of talking about race in a multicultural environment, and its impact on academic achievement for students of color. A healthy school climate depends on it.

I welcome the notion of taking the discussion a step further and taking it beyond the classroom and out into the streets, talking about race not only in the classroom but also on a community-wide level. I offer some personal thoughts on Vermont, Ruby Payne, and schools that work for all students.

Much of the empirical research on Black males and their schooling has focused on the intersection of socioeconomic status linked to aspiration and attainment within the urban environment. Research, however, has traditionally labeled students and their families at risk or in deficit, while not taking into consideration the systems of power and privilege, biased structures, and individual agency inside the institution that obstruct equity, thereby reproducing and perpetuating such abysmal outcomes.

Current research has started to take a closer look at public schooling through the lens of student experience, in turn providing valuable information to both the public and private sector on how to prepare communities and schools for students who will be bringing to the table ways of being and seeing that have their genesis in non-dominant cultural practices. Unless schools, leadership, and educators are prepared to understand the cultural differences that students bring to the classroom, the individual experiences of young people may not be as positive and meaningful as we would like them to be.

In the next chapter we will look at what the research says about the schooling of Black males through the lens of critical race theory.

Notes

1. See "John Dewey" (1959).
2. For more on Vermont's contribution to special education law, see Thousand and Villa (1995).
3. The term *Black males* will be used interchangeably to define not only African Americans (descendants of the African diaspora) but also to define African, Caribbean, and biracial Blacks.
4. New England Common Assessment Program (NECAP). "Since 2005, Vermont students have been participating in the New England Common Assessment Program (NECAP), a series of reading, writing, mathematics and science achievement tests, administered annually, which were developed in collaboration with the Rhode Island and New Hampshire departments of education. There are no native language versions of the NECAP assessments. The NECAP tests measure students' academic knowledge and skills relative to the Grade Expectations for Vermont's Framework of Standards and Learning Opportunities. Student scores are reported at four levels of academic achievement; Proficient with Distinction, Proficient, Partially Proficient and Substantially Below Proficient. Reading and math are assessed in grades 3–8 and 11, writing is assessed in grades 5, 8 and 11, and science is assessed in grades 4, 8 and 11. The reading, math and writing tests are administered each year in October. The science tests are administered in May" (http://education.vermont.gov/new/html/pgm_assessment/necap.html). For more information on the NECAP tests, see the web site listed here.
5. See United States Department of Education (2009).
6. See United States Department of Education (2009).
7. See Gay (2010), Hallinan (2008), Kunjufu (2005), and Reyes (2006).
8. For some arguments as to why Black males may not be succeeding in school, see Kunjufu (2005).
9. For more on modern racism and the notion of color blindness see Bonilla-Silva (2006).
10. For more on the history of race relations between Black males and White women, see Hancock (2006).
11. Cultural competence is the ability to relate across cultural difference. For more on cultural competence see, Delpit (1995).

12. For more on graduation rates, and Black males in Vermont, see Schott Foundation for Public Education (2010).
13. See Payne (1996) and Payne, DeVol, & Dreussi Smith (2001).
14. See, for examples, Stack (1975).
15. For more on racial microagressions in schools, see Sue, Lin, Torino, Capodilupo, and Rivera (2009).
16. For more on stereotype threat, see Steel, Spencer, & Aronson (2002).
17. For more on the Ku Klux Klan (KKK) and racism in Vermont, see Neill (1989).
18. See, United Nations (1989), "Convention on the Rights of the Child," Article 28 (Education) and Article 29 (Aims of Education).
19. For further discussion of the historical rise in racial resistance to African Americans' liberties, read *Sundown Towns* by James Loewen (2005). For discussion of the presence of the Ku Klux Klan (KKK) in Vermont at the turn of the last century, see Neill's (1989) *Fiery Crosses in the Green Mountains*.
20. For more on Vermont eugenics, see Gallagher (2001).

CHAPTER TWO

Does Race Still Matter?

In the previous chapter, I discussed the notion that data pertaining to aspiration and attainment for Black males had been hard to acquire, due to the complex nature of local district practices in formulating data that capture race and gender as a stand-alone disaggregate (i.e., Black males). Also, in tandem to that notion, the fact that there actually exists an evidenced history of racial intolerance in the state and racial bullying and harassment in Vermont public schools speaks of widespread inaction on the part of both decision makers and the lack of urgency in responding to race-based bullying and harassment. The message was clear when the 2009 Youth Risk Behavior Survey (YRBS) data informed us that students of color were still having negative school experiences (Vermont Department of Health, 2009).

Moreover, these compelling and complex issues based in history along with a predominance of liberal color blindness, and a reluctance to engage in conversations about race in transformative ways, tell me that we still have a long way to go in achieving equity and social justice for some students of color. Indeed, race still matters, even in this era of "post-civil rights." Please do not misread my critical perspective. It stems from my sense of urgency as well as seeing the big picture. I realize that it is true that members of the community have come together in the past to hold much needed discussions about race. It is also true that data have been intentionally gathered in order to look at disparities in race and policing. I applaud the efforts of the Office of Civil Rights (OCR) and local municipalities' due diligence on these issues. Especially around race-based incidents in the schools across the state that included teachers' lack of response or slow reaction to many incidents revealed by the young men who share their schooling experiences. However, it has been predominantly White liberals and some people of color who find these conversations and issues unimportant. First we might want to ask how that can be and why?

These points may be barriers across race, and are likely contributing factors in keeping people from coming together.

Years ago, many people of color, along with a few allies throughout the state, expressed their concerns about the negative experiences they had with bigotry and institutionalized racism. The conversations focused on health, education, housing, and economics, all of which continue to be symptomatic of perpetual injustice in our social sphere today. In my discussion, I also offered a historical framework for analysis on how dynamics of the new racism of color blindness continue to be a barrier in actualizing an even playing field for some students in our public schools. Moreover, the shadowy side of the green mountains—its history of racism dating back to the turn of the last century, as well as a history of racism in its public schools—has provided a baseline of evidence from which to investigate the possibility that race may still matter in school today, even in liberal, progressive Vermont. Hegemony remains an entrenched issue in many of the nations institutions and here in Vermont public schools as well, in terms of both policy and practice. Unless White privilege and color-blind practices are examined and challenged, they will continue to be barriers to actualizing equity for traditionally bypassed students. Hence, what we are charged with as education leaders, advocates and activists is to strive on behalf of those who have been rendered invisible and silenced.

A few Black males mention that while attending a variety of public schools throughout the state of Vermont, they have experienced practices that have impacted not only their ability to have a meaningful school experience, but also their future opportunities. Factors such as discipline practice, suspensions, non-inclusive curricula, cultural mismatch with some White teachers, overuse of special education, and low-level tracking, as well as teachers' expectations have impeded their access and opportunity (Kunjufu, 2005) as students. These factors contribute to the reality that some African American males have had less than stellar public schooling experiences regardless of their social class.

I believe that until the color-blind elephant in the middle of the room becomes clearly visible and acknowledged, some schools across the state may not be able to meet the needs and aspirations of the students of color who will be in attendance. Engaging in community-wide conversation about race is a beginning in the quest to bring equity to the table of social justice. Before that can happen however, hierarchies of privilege must be dismantled, and the distancing behaviors which can be very silencing, disempowering, and prohibitive to the process and actualization of equity must willingly be discarded. In other words its not only about class here in Vermont, its also about race as well.

In this chapter, I will discuss why race still matters, by utilizing the lens of critical race theory (CRT) to look at what the body of research-based literature has to say about the schooling experiences of students of color and Black males in general. To start, I will deconstruct the notion of race in the context of our nation's history, then define critical race theory, and discuss current literature on CRT and its relevance to twenty-first-century education.

I will further discuss CRT's relationship to perceptions around cultural difference, special education, and zero tolerance policy, as well as its relationship to suspensions and expulsions. The impact of teachers' attitudes, beliefs, and assumptions about Black males, and their expectations for student achievement and success are factors, which are highly critical for the realization of equitable policies and practices. With a long history of subordinated relations in America, the achievement gap in school is a reflection of Blacks' historic social status in America, which runs along both race and class lines. In order to gain a deeper understanding of the racialized society in which we live, we must first take into account the construction of race and its role in upholding hegemonic norms—how it became systemic in institutions and socially salient in the consciousness of the dominant culture.

Race Is Not Real, However, Racism Is

An ideology of race has created one of the greatest contradictions in the history of America. Historically, freedom and liberty were at the center of the conundrum. Today, opportunity and justice are tied up in the history as well. The creation of race and its far-reaching effects in America has its roots in the capitalist elite mind-sets of both Europe and the colonies, dating back to the seventeenth century.[1]

What are social constructions according to race or skin color? How are they created, by whom, and for what purpose? What are the impacts and costs of such on the society during the post-civil rights era?

According to social scientists, notions of race were created to serve the purpose of categorizing people in the social order of a hierarchic society where privilege and power are accorded to an individuals' racial, ethnic and/or class identity.[2] Constructs such as race are influenced by the ideologies and value systems embraced by those with the social power to create them. To gain an understanding of race as a modern construct, we must first investigate the evolution of race as a historical phenomenon (Fields, 2001). In her account of the relationship between freedom and race in America on the eve of the Revolution, Dr. Barbara Fields, posits in a presentation to the filmmakers and producers of the documentary "Race the Power of an Illusion," that "freedom was the central issue in the debate about colonial self-rule. Freedom and servitude we intricately bound and once race based slavery was established along with the social justifications for it, non-whites became raced people" (Race the Power of an Illusion, 2001). Therefore exploited Africans were pawns for Whites to use in order to break ties with the Crown. Once an inferior status was established and confirmed Blacks then remained at the bottom of a social hierarchy that condemned them and their progeny to generational oppression and dehumanization regardless of free status or not (Horton & Horton, 2005). Whites gained a status based on skin color, which elevated them regardless of social class.

America's primary notions of race were based on English colonial law. An emerging construction of race in America served the purpose of maintaining a caste system of political, social, and economic apartheid in service to the growing needs of a slave-based economy. Furthermore, free markets required the exploitation of mass labor. Sugar and cotton were the money producing commodities of the time, and production required an intense amount of human resources. Initially indentured of all colors participated as labor to rich landowners. On the eve of the revolution, stolen Africans provided ready, cost-free labor. Hence, exploiting Africans—and justifying it because of skin color—made economic sense. The concept of race was a foreign notion in what historian Ira Berlin names, the early Atlantic world (Horton & Horton, 2005, p. 19). People identified with their countries of native origin. Names identified and signified both place and culture: Atlantic Creole names such as, Anthony Portuguese, or Antonio de Angola, were identifiers marking the bearers of these names as people of color who most likely had connections to Africa, Europe, and the colonies (Berlin, 1998, p. 23). Their names were Christian names, which defined their intercultural connection to the European world (Berlin, 1998). Atlantic Creoles were non-raced and unfettered by lifelong bondage. Moreover, many also held status as free people. Skin color was of little or no significance. Nevertheless, their multiracial status put many on the margins, even though they were highly valued for their multicultural skills (Berlin, 1998, p. 22). Their skills as interpreters and navigators proved valuable to the companies and individuals setting up a presence in the Western Atlantic world.

Some Creoles, along with Whites in the colonies, were indentured servants. Both African and European indentured servants worked until they earned freedom, which was outlined in the terms of their contracts (Berlin, 1998). In a sense Atlantic Creoles had the same limitations in their status as indentured servants, in a hierarchy based on social and class status.

The colonies however, were influenced by policy and laws mandated by the English Parliament. During the early years, the law was very ambiguous, which actually benefited exploited Africans, making it possible for them to find freedom through arguing the ambiguous loopholes within the colonial legal system (Berlin, 1998, p. 25).

The first mention of race and connections to the law appeared on the books when the British made a distinction according to skin color in the mid-seventeenth century. By 1638, an exploited, captive, African woman's condition affected her children's status as well. Therefore a child born to a woman who held a captive status was also labeled a slave (Horton & Horton, 2005; see also Higginbotham, 1978). Laws that enforced perpetual exploitation and servitude through matrilineal lines also acted to exonerate White men who sired children with exploited, captive, African women (Smedley, 1999). White men did not have to recognize the children they sired in the slave quarter. The Black community, however, accepted many children born of these circumstances, even though the White world often disowned them (Smedley, 1999, p. 32). By 1667, Parliament began making laws that were explicit only to race. Moreover, notions of race in terms of its social construction began to develop as Britain's involvement in the Atlantic slave trade became essential to the country's economic development (Horton & Horton, 2005). By 1667, Parliament began making laws that were explicit only to race.

The eighteenth century was a crucial period for the conceptualization of distinct races, and the socialization of the idea of the racial inferiority of African Americans in the psyche of White America (Horton, 2005). Founding father and framer of the Declaration of Independence Thomas Jefferson, who idealized the notion of freedom and democracy, was extremely narrow-sighted, because today, even two hundred years later, concepts of race are still a nightmare in the form of institutionalized inequality based on race.

Jefferson's notion of the inferiority of Black people is documented in his work entitled, *Notes on the State of Virginia*. Here is a classic example of a White man with privilege and power creating the mythology of race and the inferiority of peoples of African descent at the same time. The scientific notion of "racial classification" was finding its place in institutions during the "Age of Enlightenment." It is apparent that Thomas Jefferson initiated the construct of racial inferiority as a way to justify race-based slavery, while at the same time applauding the greatness of democracy and freedom. During the Revolutionary period the drive to justify the inhuman institution of slavery led policymakers of the time to explore notions of race. Thomas Jefferson defined what he believed were the innate differences amongst the races in a lesser known work of his, writing of a "suspicion" that Blacks were inferior to Whites (Jefferson, 1781/1982,p. 86). He further asserts, in his suspicions "compares them by their faculties of memory, reason, and imagination, it appears [to me], that in memory they are equal to the whites; in reason much inferior, as I think one could scarcely be found capable of tracing and comprehending the investigations of Euclid; and that in imagination they are dull, tasteless, and anomalous (Jefferson, 1781/1982, p.143).

Jefferson's conjectures on Black inferiority, fueled errant views that have dehumanized generations of African Americans since his book was first published. Jefferson could not substantiate his "notions" because they lacked scientific proof. However, the world of eighteenth-century science attempted to confirm his imaginings. Scientists of the early eighteenth century attempted to advance Jefferson's allegations: the methodology used to try and prove his assumptions that race was based in biology were unscientific, yet they were widely accepted as fact (Smedley, 1999). His suppositions about the innate inferiority of Black people had the cachet of science and drew on respect for Jefferson to establish them as true. White people's acceptance of such flawed tenets has caused problems for our nation and has been at the root of racial injustice for African Americans and other people of color, since.

When the founding fathers were framing the Declaration of Independence, the conundrum of race occupied much of their background reflection. Creating constructs to justify African low social status became the focus of Jeffersonian ideology. It was the freedom of European colonials from British tyranny that sealed the fate of millions of African American people for generations. Generating a social construction of race was the rationale for the justification of having people in bondage, because their free labor built the economies of both Europe and the Americas (Horton & Horton, 2005). Jefferson's dehumanizing depictions of Blacks painted a picture of their inferiority, belittling their capacities, intelligence, and character (Jefferson, 1781/1982, p. 87). An ideology of race gave permission to devalue people of color and place them on the lower rung in the human family. Furthermore, the Black codes of the mid-seventeenth century attested to the brutality bestowed on exploited Africans by people who identified themselves as Christian (Berlin, 1998, p. 23). Black codes defined Black space, rights, and freedom of movement. Laws with race designations were passed all over the colonies. Laws that affected the freedom of movement and social subjugation of free Blacks as well (McIntyre, 1993). During the height of the institution of slavery, it was against the law in slaveholding states for Blacks to get an education.[3] To understand the implications of racism and its effects on the safety of students of color we need a baseline understanding of the history of racism and violence in America's public schools.

Education historian, Lawrence Cremin said, "Educational history is the history of all institutions that have shaped American thought and character, including families, churches, libraries, museums, publishers, newspapers, and benevolent societies" (Cremin, 1980, as cited in Spring, 2008, p. 20). The American public school was founded on European ethics, customs, and ideologies.

The struggle for equity in the society and the school has been a bitter and at times violent fight for students marginalized by race, class, and gender.

In *Deculturalization and the Struggle for Equality: A Brief History of Education of Dominated Groups in the United States*, education historian, Joel Spring acknowledged that "Violence and racism are a basic part of American history and of the history of the school" (Spring, 2010, p. 2). Keeping slaves ignorant was the slaveholders' goal. In *The American School From the Puritans to No Child Left Behind* (2008), Spring further asserts, "Resistance to educating slaves was rooted in fear that education would give them access to ideas that would cause slave rebellions and threaten the institution of slavery" (p. 29). During the antebellum period, African and African American slaves were banned from obtaining an education in both the South and North alike. Educational racism became institutionalized and violence was the practice to keep subordination in check. Intimidation was used to bar Blacks from the privileges and benefits that were viewed as the sole rights of the White population. Slaves covertly learning to read knew it could cost them a limb or even their lives if they were discovered. Free Blacks also had to endure the effects of living in a racist society, and had to fight for the right to freedom of movement, educational justice, and equality for their children. Access to education was available to a few: fewer still could afford tuition.

In 1849 a groundbreaking case in the Boston, Massachusetts, public school system, *Roberts vs. Boston* (Spring, 2008, p. 120) put an end to racism against freed Blacks in Boston. Other court challenges over the years have forced equal public access to education nationwide, for every child. However, years of exclusion created enormous social, economic, and opportunity gaps in our school systems that still keep in place and perpetuate an unequal playing field for students of color. Spring (2008) stated, "unequal education means unequal opportunities" (p.118).

With emancipation at the end of the Civil War, followed by Reconstruction, African Americans made rapid advances in acquiring economic stability and upward mobility through education, self-determination, and group uplift.

Representation in the political organizations of the nation and the acquisition of literacy uplifted the group with undeniable hope and resources for self-reliance. Former slaveholders were not happy with the gains African Americans were making, particularly in education, because proof that access to education could benefit oppressed groups contradicted everything the dominant culture was socialized to believe about Black people and "others."

The rise of violence directed toward Blacks made school an exciting yet vulnerable and deadly place. In 1896, "separate but equal" was good enough for the courts. Thus, segregated schools were sanctioned legally, propagating the segregationist laws known as "Jim Crow" (Spring, 2008, p. 117). These laws perpetuated White supremacy and legitimized the notion of the "inferiority" of African Americans. "Segregated education was intended to reinforce among many European Americans a belief in their own superiority over African Americans and other non-whites" (Spring, 2008, p 307). This goal has been at the center of education debate since the genesis of public education and access by non-Whites.

During this time, the majority of African Americans had access to education. Segregated education was often substandard and focused on preparing African Americans to remain on the lower end of the social and economic hierarchy in order to maintain the status quo. Any attempt to uplift the cause for Black students was met with dominance, debate, and at times violence. "Segregation translates into maintaining white supremacy and authority" (Spring, 2004, p. 48). The landmark case of *Brown v. Board of Education of Topeka, Kansas* (p. 47) made the segregation of public institutions illegal in America. Opening the doors of White schools to Black students, however, created deep conflicts and tensions between groups, which had been divided by laws, socialized stereotypes, and distortions for centuries. During this time, blood was shed in numerous "riots and killings over school integration which lasted from the 1950s to the 1970s" (Spring, 2004, p. 115). This aspect of education wars has been one in which the struggle has been a long clash of competing cultural ideologies. The essential struggle has been one for White cultural supremacy and dominance and equity and justice.

One of the best ways for any culture to transfer its cultural ideologies is through the school and the curriculum. Public school systems are adept at delivering hegemony through exclusion of the voice of others in the curriculum as well as ranking and sorting students for their social roles in social hierarchy. Schools play a central role in the distribution of particular knowledge in a society based on a student's social class (Anyon, 1981). The curriculum is driven and continues to be driven by a set of standards that only values one kind of knowledge and that is the knowledge and values of the groups who hold the power (Apple, 1993). Apparently within this paradigm the most powerful members of the community make individual and school policy decisions that ignore distort or do not fully represent the heritage and perspectives of all of the community's students.

Racism within the curriculum meant that the voice, history, beliefs, and values of traditionally bypassed groups were excluded from the national narrative. In the classrooms of White America students are taught from the perspective of a male, Eurocentric view. The curriculum was explicit in the maintenance of rigid, conservative ethics, patriotism, conformity, Western moral ethics, and cultural dominance. Since emancipation, people of African descent had to continually struggle to overcome socialized attitudes and beliefs about their intelligence and human dignity. After Reconstruction, former exploited, captive Africans were denied the right to education. In addition to such lack of access, the right to life, liberty, and the pursuit of happiness was perpetually in delicate balance, by oppressive laws and violent opposition to their status as freed people. The curriculum, when available, was prepared for them, in order to maintain their second-class status (Watkins, 2001). They were taught housekeeping and carpentry skills that would perpetuate Black subordination to Whites (Watkins, 2001).

Hence, hundreds of years of racial injustice have been the legacy for multiple generations of Black people. The process was institutionalized through laws that barred Blacks from fair housing, education, health care, and equal protection under the law. Needless to say, the school system was used to perpetuate these inequities through the implementation of policy and practices that have entrenched racist structures and systems up until today.

Moreover, Jim Crow laws reinforced the constructs of Black inequality. Separate and unequal was the normative practice with regard to access to education and other public accommodations for Blacks. Denial of citizenship was one way of implementing race-based injustice (Fireside, 2004). Regardless of education (at best mediocre and lacking the basic essentials), Black people still strove to become educated despite White opposition.

Education historian James D. Anderson highlighted the fact that "upon emancipation the first constitutional right that newly freed Blacks sought and demanded more than anything else was for access to an education" (Anderson, 1988, p. 25). On the eve of emancipation, it was observed that the Black community had established its own schools in lieu of waiting for White allies from the north to help them (Williams, 2005). Between 1860 and 1865, more than 500 "native schools" (administered and run by Blacks) were already in operation (Williams, 2005, p. 98). However, the power of local and state rights, especially under the yoke of racial apartheid in the South, considered this demand and desire as an opportunity to enforce oppressive and marginalizing policy that was in line with the social and political ideologies of the era, an era defined by White supremacy (Watkins, 2001). The reigning policy spoke to what was assumed to be an "innate inferiority" in the capacities of Black people to govern not only themselves but also their community at large (Williams, 2005, p. 13). This pattern of assumed lack of adequacy on the part of Black people was maintained to perpetuate old antebellum social and political boundaries. The challenge for education equality was not just the problem in the south. Access to equal education also was problematic in the north as well.

Today's schools, therefore, have not fully entered into the new millennium because traditionally held values and beliefs are still normative in policy as well as practice. Social reproduction theory states that schools (where cultural pluralism may be part of the social order) implement social structures to serve and thus uphold hierarchies of class, race, and gender (Bowles, 1975). Social institutions within the society help to maintain hierarchies through valuing and rewarding hegemonic norms. Moreover, Jean Anyon (1981) in an essay published in *Curriculum Inquiry*, vol. 11, no. 1, Spring 1981. states, "The curriculum is matched to students class and social status (Anyon, 1981, p. 38). The working-class curriculum to the elite curriculum are part and parcel of the racist and classist ideologies that drive schools even today, to pigeon hole students into the same social class status as their parents (p. 38).[4]

Knowledge is socially and ideologically constructed (Sadovnik, 1991), in order to serve the best interest of the dominant class (Bowles

& Gintis, 1976). Constructs of race, class, and gender help to uphold and maintain socioeconomic, political, and racial supremacy, all aspects of the status quo (Apple, 1995) while capitalism perpetuates these inequities as well (Bowles & Gintis, 1976).

If we look beyond the borders of our own national issue of race, we can see that it is also a global issue. Racial apartheid in both America and South Africa are a prime example of the phenomenon in our contemporary time (Walker & Archung, 2003). It is not necessary to read dusty texts from Jefferson to see that racism still persists today. The important point is to find a way to change people's thinking and behaviors and to work toward making racism disappear so that all Americans are truly considered as equals and are treated equally.

Competing ideologies that only serve the powers that be are in the way of true educational justice. The only way we can create truly equitable schools is to understand that as citizens we must have the moral courage to critique and question the systems that oppress us. In order to change unjust institutions, we must be willing to challenge old assumptions and define new meanings. The current reforms in education seek to make schools more just and inclusive, yet it could be argued that progress has been stalled—even, reversed. No Child Left Behind (Vinovskis, 2009; "No Child Left Behind," 2009) is a noble and lofty ideal, yet it still holds social reproduction at the front of the agenda. Reforms that only value hegemony will not meet the needs of all students and will surely leave far too many behind.

Needless to say, rigor is important in school, but relevancy is more important especially if non-White students are to find meaning in their education. Students need to find meaning in what they do in school, including in relationships with their teachers, because mutual respect is at the center of these relationships. Regardless of race mutual respect and a level of cultural competence are a requirement. We must talk about all the issues that create barriers to our students succeeding. We will be unable to effect change if we do not keep the conversation of race on the table. To avoid the dialogue is to render it invisible. Even though ideologies about race have persisted throughout history, I believe they can be changed. The field of anthropology announced in 1992 that it would henceforth disregard race as biology. Biology and the field of genetics have deconstructed the scientific notions of race within the past few decades.[5] Nevertheless, it's now up to society to deconstruct or dismantle the social side with students, in our schools. That is what justice can look like.

Gandhi once said, "If we want true peace, we must start with the children." To start with the children, however, we must also look to those who are not only caring for them but, those who are also teaching them. The world community has the power to change the paradigm and facilitate the freedom that true equity creates by continuing this conversation. As activists and advocates, we owe it to the future. The conversation, starting from the top down, is essential in changing the climate and culture of the school, which translate into achievement for students of color. The ability of those in charge to understand the new faces of color on a level of competence will send the message to the children that the school is both caring and just. Perhaps, we can start by looking at race, education, leadership, and transformation through a lens of critical race theory.

Definition of Critical Race Theory

Since the 1970s critical race theorists suggest that White supremacy is a common rather than an unusual feature of American society, affecting marginalized groups in all of its sectors (Delgado, 1995, p. xiv). Furthermore, White supremacy's salience in American life and institutions has been theorized in the body of literature on law, ethnic studies, political science, and education (p. xiii). Critical race theorists challenge the dominant discourse on race and racism as it interacts and relates to the intersections of both class and gender with institutional power. Approaches were gravely needed to understand and come to terms with the more subtle (but just as deeply entrenched) varieties of liberal racism that characterize life in postmodern times (p. xv).

Moreover, CRT has multiple themes or principles that are addressed in the literature. The notion of objectivity is another barrier to racial justice because it circumvents any potential dialogue that may provide grounds for dealing with racial incidents. The silence produced by color blindness prevents Blacks from naming their reality or the covert acts of racism in the daily assaults on their humanity and dignity. The use of storytelling and counter-storytelling is one of the most common features in naming one's reality in qualitative methodology, such as in this text.

Furthermore, CRT challenges liberal ideologies that promote color blindness. Color blindness, a remnant of the overt racism of the "Jim Crow" era, allows racism to continue in covert, subtle, institutional, and non-racial ways.[6] The notion of color blindness traces its origins to the words of Justice Harlan in his 1896 dissent in the landmark case *Plessy v. Ferguson:* Where he argued that "Justice was blind and race should not matter."[7]

Supremacy ideologies exist solely in order to keep power and privilege in place. This new ideology of color blindness has emerged to defend the contemporary racial order of color-blind racism (Bonilla-Silva, 2006, p. 25). Central to color blindness refers to the notion of blaming the victims for their social, cultural, and economic circumstances. Bonilla-Silva further argues that these ideologies are expressions at the symbolic level of dominance. The new racism of color blindness has four frames—abstract liberalism, naturalization, cultural racism, and the minimization of racism—anchored for the interpretation of these new racial ideologies. Abstract liberalism (Bonilla-Silva, 2006) tends to hold the greatest capital because it is at the foundation of color blindness (p. 25). Thus, old notions of race and racism have morphed into a ubiquitous, yet invisible, way of keeping racial dominance in place (p.25).

This dichotomous logic of White supremacy is at the center of our nation's social, economic, and political inequities prevailing today, including in our schools, where race is normally discussed in the frame of color blindness when dealing with non-White students. We cannot serve students of color if we are blind to their racial, ethnic, and cultural identities.

Early scholarship inquiring into the social condition of Black America started by looking through the lens of race (Du Bois, 1903/1993; Woodson, 1933/1990). Early data showed gaps in all sectors of society: health, economics, housing, and education. Furthermore, the normative lens for the sociological analysis of Blacks had been theorized through the concept of deficit theory (Herrnstein & Murray, 1994). Deficit theory blamed the "Black condition" on Black intellectual capacity, positing this as inherent in the social condition. It thus misdirected the blame, failing to place it where it needed to be focused: on the systems and structures produced by White supremacy culture.

Both conservatives and liberals alike have held as gospel this very provincial view of defining non-Whites as intellectually and morally deficient. For example, Black conservative, John McWhorter, made the case that Blacks undermine their own progress and success by embracing a mind-set of "victimization," making it less likely that Black students will take school seriously (McWhorter, 2000). McWhorter felt that "slight transgressions by Whites do not qualify as racism." (p. 2) Instead, he claimed that "anti-intellectualism" is the barrier to Black academic success and achievement (McWhorter, 2000, p. 83). On the one hand, McWhorter's conservative position aligns with aversive views that many Whites hold about people of color and their status as second-class citizens. I get the impression that McWhorter believes that racism is an issue of the past. Moreover, McWhorter's assumption that Blacks do not value education is shortsighted, to say the least. On the other hand, there are threads of truth to his claims that cannot be denied, such as poverty and fatherlessness, which complicate the lives of some students. The claim, however, overlooks or even fails to consider the institutional structures that have a history of marginalizing African Americans (especially males), prohibiting them from being gainfully employed and parenting their children. Hence, McWhorter's claims are shortsighted and work to promote color blindness, thus keeping aversive racism in place. His opinion absolves White people of their guilt and reinforces an unearned place for them as privileged people socialized to believe in others' assumed defects. He further claimed that the cause of this lack of measurable achievement is not racism, inadequate school funding, class status, or a parent's educational level. He claims "anti-intellectualism" in the Black community as the culprit (McWhorter, 2000). He articulated this idea by comparing immigrant and other minority achievement experiences to those of Black Americans. This lack of seeing the issues of race and racism in the school as systemic and structural does not give him a basis to stand on.

Moreover, to minimize Black students' experiences when it comes to the daily micro assaults (Sue, Lin, Torino, Capodilupo, & Rivera, 2009) and stereotype threats (Steel, Spencer, & Aronson, 2002) on their humanity is in itself a form of color blindness. To claim they are not race-based is to discount one's reality and to marginalize the voice of those who are victimized by such acts. To say that voluntary minorities are immune to the racism that exists in our country is despicable, to say the least. Voluntary minorities and involuntary minorities carry a different status in America due to the history of exploitation and captivity of Africans and their descendants (Ogbu, 1987). Hundreds of years of racial injustice and subordination in America can make even the most conservative minority suspect at times. African Americans were continually at the bottom of the social and economic hierarchy, and deficit theories claiming Black inferiority made it easy for racist systems to work at leaving Blacks there. Those systems worked because of the unquestioned and thus invisible norms that drive hegemony. Deficit thinking undermines and hinders students' progress and success in school. Hence, critical race theory is an empowering framework that facilitates the deconstruction of the condition of African American males being educated within public school systems.

Critical Race Theory of Education

Critical race theory of education entered into the body of social science literature in the mid-1990s (Ladson-Billings & Tate, 1995). The arguments related to equity were drawn from the early judicial literature from which critical race theory emerged (Bell, 1992). Critical race theory has at least five themes: the intersections of race and racism, the challenge to the dominant ideology, the commitment to social justice, the centrality of experiential knowledge, and the interdisciplinary perspective that insists on analyzing race and racism by placing them in a historical and contemporary context using interdisciplinary methods (Delgado, 1995; Bell, 1992).

Considerable research had been conducted in the field of sociology in explaining the significance of race in the context of American society (Omi & Winant, 1994). By using race as an analytical tool, researchers concur that race is a matter of both social structure and cultural representation in the school setting (Ladson-Billings & Tate, 1995). Ladson-Billings and Tate argued on the same grounds as their theoretical predecessors that schooling inequities are a logical and predictable result of the racialized society that defines America and its socio-cultural arrangements according to skin color (Ladson-Billings & Tate, 1995, p. 47).

Along with Bell and Delgado, they acknowledged that their research was built on the earlier body of knowledge produced by both Du Bois (1903/1993) and Woodson (1933/1990), whose theories worked to countervail the pathological inferiority thinking inculcated by racist theorists at the turn of the last century. By using the same theoretical framework, the modern research attempted to break up and decipher the social-structural and cultural significance of race in education, and its effect on student wellbeing, access, and achievement (Ladson-Billings & Tate, 1995).

Another proposition posited by CRT about education is the notion of property rights. Since the attainment of property and the resulting ownership was a salient sign of status for White men in the new republic, the ownership of humans as property became a prime aspect of White supremacy. What Ladson-Billings and Tate argued is that property rights in the form of intellectual property are one of the most contested issues around curriculum in the education of students of color living in a racially dominant society. Multiculturalism and traditional education are the culture wars that have been at the center of school reform debates for the past twenty years.[8]

The contest is wrapped up in of whose knowledge is valued in the classroom as well as portrayed in texts and lessons is central to the argument on property rights and its relationship to official knowledge represented in the curriculum (Apple, 1995).

An analysis of the issues facing African American males is an appropriate method for understanding the school experiences of African American males in predominantly White communities. Looking at schooling through the framework of critical race theory can offer us insight into how to address the issues that emerging populations of color face in these communities.

The following subchapters express the individual factors or domains that affect the educational outcomes of African American males in public schools across the nation. Disparities in schools according to race and gender are centered around discipline policy and practice, special education, access to educational enrichment, as well as the cultural competence of predominantly White administrators and teaching staff.

Black Boys and Special Education

Black boys have been systematically programmed to fail by the time they reach the fourth grade (Kunjufu, 2005, p. v). To be a Black male in America means that one is most likely to be defined by the socially constructed negative stereotypes that characterize Black boys as dangerous, dumb, deprived, deviant, and disturbed due to a conspiracy in school systems that destroy them by burdening them with the remnants of a racist society (p. iv).

School failure can also be connected to teachers who are predominantly White and middle-class and who are failing Black boys because of the racist structures that prevail in the schools (p. 83). Eighty percent of the U.S. teaching force is comprised of White women (National Education Association (NEA), 2010) and Black men comprise only 1% (National Education Association (NEA), 2010) of the teaching force. By default, this lack of balance is a mix for disaster because too many of these White, female teachers do not have contact with communities of color outside of the classroom. Their middle-class status creates a barrier in both the social and cultural spheres of the students they teach. Moreover, the combination of biased curricula, a lack of Black, male teacher role models, and White teachers who see Black, male students as incapable rather than able, makes it difficult for Black male students to hold their own (Kunjufu, 2005).

In addition, often Black boys are ill-prepared to survive in an educational system that marginalizes them through omission in the curriculum, disciplines and suspends them for nonviolent transgressions, and tracks them to low-level classes (p. v). When Black students neither know their culture nor themselves; they are vulnerable to the effects of racism (p. v). While self-esteem may be an issue, other factors, too, contribute to the problem. Many middle-class teachers are culturally disconnected from the African American students they teach. Color blindness and cultural incompetence are mitigating factors that affect even the brightest of African American students, dooming them to becoming a statistic to unjust outcomes.

Many White teachers do not know what to do with students of color, particularly Black boys. Therefore, they are more inclined to put them in special education classes for perceived behavioral and cognitive issues (p. v). Furthermore, special education is often the first place where Black boys find their first negative experience in school. Thirty-three percent of special education students are African American males who are disproportionately tracked to nonacademic classes compared to their White peers (Kunjufu, 2005). African Americans make up only 17% of the overall student population nationwide, yet they are lagging way behind their White counterparts academically. Statistics tell us that even White males in poverty achieve academically on par with middle-class African American males (Gabriel, 2010).

Kunjufu further states that the stigma associated with special education is that it has its own set of labels. Many of the labels serve to reinforce stereotypes and further create barriers to achievement (p. 8). Moreover, these stereotypes impede access to just and equitable education because teachers' assumptions are informed by such labels—negative labels which follow Black boys throughout most of their educational careers and often into their adult lives as well. Hence, the conspiracy to destroy Black boys is believed by some, to be fueled by White supremacy culture, through domination of our educational institutions (p. v). However, we need to ask, "What about Black males from middle-class families who are not burdened by fatherlessness, violence in their communities, and who attend high-achieving schools that are predominantly White?" Even when habitus (Bourdieu, 1977) is apparent within the home environment and perceived to most likely ensure success—such as having two highly educated parents and access to social and economic capital—it is still not uncommon for even middle-class Black males to get caught up in the wheel of injustice in school. Injustice makes it hard to achieve and in some cases, if Black male students do graduate, they often find it difficult to achieve in the academy and graduate from college as well (Allen, 2010). Unjust discipline policy and practice targeted toward moving males of color outside the school and interfering with their access to education and a positive future, represents an injustice, one of the unintended consequences of structural racism. Policy and practice dictate that once these young men become caught up in the cycle, the negative consequences will follow many of them throughout their adult lives making them vulnerable to the negative outcomes many young Black and Hispanic men are facing today.

When this country began to see dramatic declines in the graduation rates of African American males starting about two decades ago, interest reemerged in understanding the gaps in achievement between White and Black students. According to the Schott Foundation's "Black Boy Report," the statistics on Vermont showed that for every three White male students admitted to district gifted and/or talented programs only approximately one Black male student was admitted. Nearly twice as many Black male students as White male students were classified as mentally retarded (Schott Foundation for Public Education, 2010, p. 3). What does this "finding" mean for Black boys in Vermont? If they are graduating in high numbers that are alleged to have created an inverted gap, then how and why are they overrepresented in special education, harshly disciplined, and suspended at high rates? As a community, we must take a closer look at the root causes in order to understand these disparities showing up in the data.

Black Boys and School Discipline

Three young males are playing a game of dice on school property. A teacher comes over to break up the game. The students notice the teacher coming their way and all three start running and scatter in different directions. With the help of another teacher, they chase after only one of the students, while the other two run off without being pursued. The student the teachers follow is Black, whereas the other two are White. When the young, Black male is caught, he is disciplined and suspended, and the two White males are free of any punitive action. (Field notes)

Inequity such as the one pointed out in the note above, occurs on a daily basis in schools across the nation. Why is there such a difference in the meting out of discipline? The reason is that there is a discipline crisis nationwide, and it is African American males and other students of color who are in trouble in school (Monroe, 2005). African American males do not suffer from some innate pathology. However, the measure to which they are disciplined is disproportionate in comparison to the degree their White peers are punished. This disconnection starts in school through the enforcement of school discipline policy with punitive practice guided by stereotypical thinking on the part of the enforcer.

Once Black boys leave the confines of the family and go to school, the downward spiral begins for some as early as the first grade (Monroe, 2005). Does labeling Black boys as "bad" set them up to fulfill the prophecy of their assumed unworthiness? Do teachers verbalize this idea of their "worthlessness" directly to students?

In her cutting-edge book *Bad Boys: Public Schools in the Making of Black Masculinity*, Ann Ferguson sheds light on some of the racialized thinking and behaviors of adults, both Black and White, who verbalize their flawed perceptions of Black criminality in boys as young as five (Ferguson, 2001). In an entry from her field notes, she wrote of an adult in a school who, while leading her on a tour, pointed out a Black youth in the hallway. He matter-of-factly said to her, "That one has a jail cell with his name on it" (Ferguson, 2001, p. 1). He was describing a ten-year-old Black male on his way to what the children in the school labeled "the punishing room."

Some adults are not as blatant as the person depicted in Ferguson's descriptive opening; however, they are out there. It is done routinely, as we can see by the apparent disproportionately high number of Black boys disciplined for nonviolent incidents. For example, they may be penalized, for nonthreatening behaviors—such as how they may dress—or be perceived as criminals by their teachers (Skiba & Rausch, 2006).

These kinds of inequities occur through unjust discipline practices such as suspension and expulsion for minor offenses. The research goes further to tell us that punitive response to Black students' transgressions were unequal to the reaction to poor behavior on the part of their White counterparts. More specifically, Black males are likely to receive the highest degree of punitive action for their behavior (Skiba & Rausch, 2006). The notion of Black male criminality may also be a big part of the equation.

The misconception of Black criminality informs teachers' perceptions as well as their expectations of Black students as being troublesome and "bad." The disconcerting aspect is that there is no research whatsoever that supports the notion that Black and Latino students act out and misbehave more than White students (Adams, 2008, p. 30).

During the 1990s, researchers began following the trend toward unequal treatment closely. In her essay, "Why Are Bad Boys Always Black? Causes of Disproportionality in School Discipline and Recommendations for Change researcher Carla R. Monroe cited earlier studies linking poor and Black male students' school experiences and the resulting negative outcomes such as delinquency, dropping out, and recidivism to a discipline gap (Monroe, 2005, p. 198). Monroe went on to refer to the discipline gap as an American phenomenon. Indeed, she pointed out the structures in the school that create the disparities, such as the criminalization of Black males, race, and class privilege as well as zero tolerance policies (Monroe, 2005, p. 198). When it comes to disciplining Black males, the treatment is usually harsher and more punitive than the punishment would be for the same offense if their White counterparts committed it. Thus, Black male students are more likely to be suspended or expelled, and then eventually they just drop out (Gay, 2010). Data state that dropping out leads to many burdens on society and that 85% of men within the justice system are dropouts (Justice Policy Institute, 2005). The choice by administrators to use harsh social control practices on Black males in school parallels similar disparities in our justice system. Needless to say, this behavior is situated in a history of social and racial injustice in American society. How do schools socially control Black males through discipline policy? Monroe's study further examined the factors that contribute to the over-representation of Black, male, and low-income students in incidences of school discipline, as she sought answers to overlooked questions and tried to understand how culturally based constructs such as race apply to school discipline (Monroe, 2005, p. 1).

African American males are socially, emotionally, and academically stifled in an environment that tells them they are both bad and worthless. There is an urgent need for the educators of Black and other males of color to understand how societal may inform their perceptions of African American male behaviors (Monroe, 2005). Cultural competence is an attribute imperative for teachers of the schools of the twenty-first century. They need to understand patterns based in the culture itself that inform identity as well as masculinity.

Moreover, there is a need to understand how and why teachers' views of students of color, especially males, are negative and how those perceptions mediate their disciplinary actions in the classroom (Monroe, 2005). Teachers are informed by the racialized world that they live in, and if they have been socialized to believe in Black male criminality, then their response to Black male behavior that they perceive as inappropriate will not be equitable with their response to the inappropriate behavior of other students. In my own experiences I believe it is a combination of these factors. With a history of stereotypes that portray people of color as dangerous it should be understandable why some folks still hold on to such negative views and beliefs.

Legal scholar Randall Kennedy (1997) summed up the perceptions of criminality and Blacks by positioning the issue within the context of law and history. Emancipation and Reconstruction brought into focus questions on how White society should deal with newly freed Blacks. Now that they were off the plantation, how would they be controlled? Furthermore, the reins of oppression during slavery as well as the violent slave codes did not require thinking about policing on such a wide scale. Law enforcement as an institution emerged out of the need and desire to socially control "those people" who lived under the reins of control all of their lives, including freed men and women of color (Kennedy, 1997).

Flawed ideologies about race and a connection to presumed criminality supported such moves. Policing was institutionalized to protect White people from Blacks: it certainly did not serve the purpose of keeping Blacks safe from the terror brought upon them by Whites (Kennedy, 1997). Moreover the notion of Black criminality goes back to before emancipation to the mid-1700s (McIntyre, 1993), with the concern about the movements of Black freed men and women in a nation that held the majority of Blacks in perpetual exploitation and captivity. These constructions are part and parcel of the entrenched fabric of a White supremacist society. Considering the history and notions derived from such thinking and practice as society, we bear the burdens of our nation's racial past—even today. Our schools are feeding the pipeline from classroom to jail cell through that paradigm.

Teachers need to become more aware of this fact and deliberate to prevent Black boys and all students from getting caught up in this cycle of injustice.

The intersections of race and class privilege further complicate the interactions between teacher and student (McIntyre, 1993, p. 89). It is clear that the challenges some African American males are facing in school are historically rooted in the psyche of American thinking and policy making as well as in the second-class status that Black people have endured within the social system. Hence, race and cultural background are obstacles in opening doors to opportunity through school for many African American youths. Black males are finding school a hard and unsuccessful proposition due to unjust and exclusionary social practices sponsored by institutional racism. However, even if they do stay connected to high school, many are ill prepared to make their way through the ivy halls (McWhorter, 2000) and stay there.

What does this mean for students who have a global proposition before them? Indeed, if most are not being prepared for the demands of a global environment, they will not participate in the shaping of global issues. In the age of No Child Left Behind (NCLB) mandates, the statistics are telling us that many Black and poor males are being left behind (Kozol, 2005). The disproportionate overrepresentation of Black males in the criminal justice system alone (Justice Policy Institute, 2005) has had a disastrous and overarching effect on not only Black families and their communities, but on the broader society as well.

The misperception of Black criminality is related to how zero tolerance policy (Reyes, 2006) is enacted in our schools. How do the unequal enforcement and unjust discipline practices of zero tolerance policy affect outcomes schooling experience and outcomes?

Zero Tolerance Policy and Males of Color

Dropout rates are connected to a variety of reasons and incidents within the school, such as suspensions and expulsions driven by harsh discipline practice, zero tolerance, and race and class privilege (Reyes, 2006). Statistics show that school discipline practices are harsher, more punitive, and disproportionately high among African American males (Blumenson & Nilsen, 2003) as well as males of Hispanic descent. The empirical research tells us that zero tolerance policy is a public school discipline policy that enforces mandatory consequences for student behavior without any regard for the conditions or circumstances, and with no room for understanding the individual student committing the assumed offense (Blumenson & Nilsen, 2003).

Critics of the policy say that its inflexibility, ambiguity, and lack of discretion on the part of administrative decision makers create a behavior management nightmare for students when faced with enforcement (Reyes, 2006). The biggest problem with such an ambiguous and inflexible policy is that children, even some kindergartners, have been penalized for their perceived infractions. If these data are showing us a national trend, what are the experiences of one of Vermont's most underrepresented yet rapidly growing populations? Students who are the most at risk and who are disproportionately overrepresented in zero-tolerance offenses are students of color (Reyes, 2006). The majority of these students are African American and Latino males, with girls of color following closely behind. These populations of males are also the populations most likely to drop out of school in the face of such harsh and punitive policy (Reyes, 2006, p. 5). What is the connection between high dropout rates of these populations and zero tolerance policy?

In her cutting-edge book *Discipline, Achievement, and Race: Is Zero Tolerance the Answer?* Augusta Reyes cogently explained the rationale and purpose behind zero tolerance and school discipline practices. She further asserted that the unintended consequence is the perpetuation of injustice towards students of color, particularly males (Reyes, 2006). There is something to be said about the paradox of tolerance in both American society and education policy. On the one hand, America has a deep history of intolerance to other races (Bell, 1992), yet society wants to give the impression that we have arrived at a state of embracing our pluralism, therefore race is not an issue in terms of justice. How can that occur if we assume a show of fairness, yet we make it possible for Congress to enact such ambiguous legislation? This intolerance manifests itself in institutionalized racism. In the education of students of color, schools are representative of an uneven playing field to begin with. Discipline policy and practice which gives more power to school administrators (who already hold an immense amount of social control capital), will only exacerbate the problem (Bell, 1992). Critics of the policy see zero tolerance as a means to move certain populations such as minorities out of the school and into the prison system (Bell, 1992, p. 7).

However, with growing, diverse populations—particularly in urban areas—education systems have been forced to look at how intolerance has affected the way humans handle issues as they relate to human relationships and interactions within the public sphere, and the power associated with such interactions. Furthermore, administrative policy-makers have now come to understand the value of tolerance in terms of both liability and safety when administering institutional policy.

The diversity movement of the past twenty-five years has made a strong claim for the importance of tolerance and inclusion in a pluralistic society. Some institutions, however, are caught in a dichotomy. The local policy advocates for safety, yet populations marginalized by both race and class are not safe. This scenario is evident in the implementation of zero tolerance policies in the school environment. Zero tolerance policy (ZTP) found its genesis in the US military as a way to enforce high standards and expectations of behavior and conduct for both uniformed and civilian personnel (Katzenstein & Reppy, 1999). The purpose of imposing such policy was to reduce deviant behaviors within the military, such as violence (domestic and within the ranks), sexual harassment, and alcohol and drug use (Reyes, 2006, p. 6). However, the statistics derived from drug testing mandated by this policy over a twenty-year period actually showed an increase in drug usage by 29% in 2001 (Reyes, 2006, p. 5). Why should such a failed policy be present in the school environment in the first place?

Furthermore, zero tolerance policies were incorporated into national crime prevention efforts to prevent violence and reduce crime in schools (Reyes, 2006). This set of rules derives from the first Safe Schools Act of 1993 as well as the Safe and Drug-Free Schools Act of 1986 (Casella, 2003). The policy's original purpose was to prohibit firearms and drugs within 1,000 feet of the school property (Reyes, 2006, p. 7).

Unfortunately, the way the policy has been enacted in a variety of school settings differs, making the policy overly ambiguous and leaving decisions up to the individual discretion of school administrators. Ambiguity in individual discretion of implementation, allowed the policy to become a slippery slope for school districts. While all students and the school community should be safe, it is unfortunate that the populations of color suffer the most under such ambiguous policy.

Even children of kindergarten age have been penalized by their schools' enforcement of the policy. The paradox is that these same schools are socializing them to become tolerant, caring citizens, yet they are treating them in both intolerant and inhumane ways, sometimes willing to expel them for ambiguous and at times benign reasons as well. These punitive actions show neither justice nor caring. Sometimes very young students are treated as though they are adult criminals.

Six-year-old central Florida student, Desre'e Watson, threw a tantrum that lasted about twenty minutes at school, not unusual for a kindergartner. What was unusual about Desre'e's circumstance was the way that the school handled her childish behavior (Herbert, 2007). This six-year-old was handcuffed and arrested by police called to the scene. When those involved were interviewed, the response was that "there were no options" according to the arresting police officer. "She was yelling and screaming—just uncontrollable, defiant." When asked by the reporter in an interview, "Did they ever consider her age being six?" The officer replied without a second thought, "Do you think she is the first 6-year-old we've arrested?" (Herbert, 2007). Students with well-documented emotional and health issues (distinctly different from deviant behaviors such as violence or alcohol and drug use) are not immune, even if they have a certified accommodation within the environment of the school. Students have been expelled from school for a variety of reasons that do not relate to the harsh consequences they receive. For instance, students have been shown the door out of school for things as benign as possession of Midol, Alka-Seltzer, and cough lozenges due to zero tolerance policy (Portner, 1996). Phillip Hernandez, an eleven-year-old student at a California elementary school, died due to the implementation of zero tolerance at the school he attended (Tarkan, 2002).

Hernandez did not die because he was violent, or a drug dealer, or a disruptive student. He died because he had an asthma attack and zero tolerance policy in his school district forbade that he carry his rescue medication on his person. The purpose in having rescue medication means just that: rescue during a surprise respiratory attack. Hernandez's medication was kept in the nurse's office far from his classroom. Unfortunately, the run to the nurse during an attack one day cost him his life. These are only a few out of a large number of situations in which zero tolerance policy has not fit the "assumed crime" or the "assumed perpetrator." In the case of Desre'e, where were the compassion and care? Indeed, how is it possible that the other adults present would allow this situation to escalate on their watch? Evidently, there was no adult who held all the attributes that constitute best practice in teaching and working with young children. Tolerance is a disposition that is necessary in order for one to be an effective, caring, and compassionate teacher. It seems that these important attributes were missing on all fronts in handling the six-year-old's issues that day in March 2007. One fact that stands out from the police report is that the child involved was an African American child. The report was brief, yet very descriptive, clearly stating that the offender was a "black female." Interestingly, though, the arresting officer left out the word "child" (Herbert, 2007).

The following research-based statistics reveal the unintended or intended consequences of zero tolerance policy as they relate to both responses to and consequences of Black and Hispanic males' perceived antisocial behavior in school:

1. Black students represent 17 % of enrollment nationally, but they comprise 32% of out-of school suspensions.
2. 25% of all Black male students are suspended at least once in a four-year period.
3. Black and Latino students are more likely to be referred for disciplinary action and to be disciplined.
4. Zero tolerance policies are more likely to exist in predominantly Black and Latino school districts.
5. Black and Latino students are more likely to be disciplined for minor misconduct and receive punishment disproportionate to the behavior.
6. Black and Latino students tend to be suspended for discretionary offenses, such as "defiance of authority" and "disrespect for authority" (Bireda, 2002).

How do we get school administrators to understand that race and discipline go hand in hand? Is it possible that they know but just do not care? I would like to believe, that administrators need to be informed about the intent behind federal mandates such as zero tolerance and how the policy and practice have no place in the school.

Student-perpetrated violence is not a new phenomenon, and since at least the 1970s student violence in the school has become a reality (Reyes, 2006, p. 1). During the past decade, some schools were burdened with profound violence, and federal zero tolerance policy was enacted as a response to such growing violence. It is important to keep students safe, but critics of the policy state that school discipline has traditionally been the sole domain of school administrators such as the principal and the vice principal. As Reyes has succinctly stated, "Butts, buses and books have traditionally been their administrative domains" (Reyes, 2006, p. v).

As an educator and social justice advocate, I have been deeply interested in how social policy enforced by school districts impacts the diverse populations who attend, especially poor and minority students. Furthermore, has ZTP made schools safer? If that is indeed the case, let me ask, safer for whom? Have we implied that enforcers have permission to perpetrate structural racism in the schools?

The research has been telling us that African Americans, particularly males, are still experiencing disparities by race and socioeconomic status starting in school, a dynamic that impedes their overall academic performance (Irvine, 1990). This pattern persists, even when the antisocial behavior of males of color is no different from that of their White counterparts (Gay, 2010).

I've heard of an experience when a White student was removed from the classroom for making a threat toward a teacher. This student's consequence was a meeting with the parents in the presence of the assistant principal, a good talking-to, and then sent back to in-school suspension. The thing about in-school suspension is that the student gets to keep up with the class assignments, as well as have access to academic resources with-in the school. Do not get me wrong: missing any class time is a loss for a student, but to have access to resources that may not be at home does not put students in a compromised situation academically.

All I am saying is that if this had been a transgression by a male of color, he would have been suspended on the spot and possibly would have been expelled with no questions asked. His family would have been under scrutiny, and the perception would have been, "We expect that from him." During my teaching assignments at primarily White schools, I have witnessed this type of injustice quite frequently. Hence, zero tolerance policy and its ambiguous enforcement have a distinct connection between race, school, academic achievement, and school discipline practices for students, particularly males.

Furthermore, the most current research on the correlation between levels of school discipline and prison provided by the states showed that 85% of males who drop out of high school usually end up marginally employed or unemployed (Justice Policy Institute, 2005). The same research recognized a relationship between dropping out and ending up in the criminal justice system at disproportionate rates for a large percentage of these populations. The system fails to realize that it costs less to educate a boy than to rehabilitate a man (Kunjufu, 2005).

Since these statistics are showing a relationship between success and achievement and the ability to stay connected to school for males of color nationwide, these same patterns affect emerging populations of color in a state like Vermont. The Schott report and the Children's Defense Fund both claim that disparities in suspensions are defined by both race and gender here in Vermont. How much are these figures influenced by teacher perception and expectations? Can these numbers be attributed to cultural mismatch as well?

Conclusion: Black Boys, Expectations, and White Teachers

Teachers and how they relate to their students have a strong effect on how students feel about school and if they will remain connected so that they achieve their educational goals (Hallinan, 2008, p. 271). Within the student-teacher relationship, both the expectation for the student to succeed and respect for the student's cultural background are important to achievement. America's teaching force is 87% White, and the largest percentage of the force is comprised of White women.

It is not too far-fetched to claim that a cultural mismatch exists for Black boys in classrooms led by White female teachers, and that this scenario may be one of the problems (Kunjufu, 2005). Thus, this should be considered in decisions about placements where males of color have to interact with each other.

One of the unintended consequences of *Brown v. Board of Education* was the creation of school environments where students of color and White women share dysfunctional relationships based on a history of fear, ignorance, mistrust, as well as resentment (Hancock, 2006, p. 95). These factors, in addition to the racialized nature of society, even today, are a recipe for disaster for some Black boys.

When I think back to my brothers' schooling, I recall that such negative issues with White teachers were the most destructive to their educational experiences. This observation is not meant to say that they did not have experiences with White teachers that were positive, because they did. Nonetheless, I can imagine what students of color are experiencing today in a school system fraught with racial and social inequities, especially at the hands of teachers who may have the best of intentions but who are informed and led by the internalized biases and attitudes prevalent in a supremacist society.

In this chapter, I have argued as well as evidenced through the literature of the history of race and racism and its salience in the lived, public-schooling experiences of African American males and other students of color that injustice exists in public schools—a lack of justice that has its cause in the racial identity of students.

Notes

1. For more on the complexities in defining the meaning of race and its social construction, see Fields, B. (2001). Presentation given at a "School" for the producers of RACE the Power of an Illusion, PBS—March2001editedtranscript,http://www.pbs.org/race/000_About/0 02_04-background-02-02.htm and Berlin (1998).
2. For more on the notion of social constructions, see Smedley (1999).
3. For more on education and former exploited, captive Africans, see Williams (2005).
4. For more on theories of social reproduction, see Bourdieu (1977).
5. For more on the retraction on the notions of race, see Smedley (1999).
6. For a cogent and clear explanation of color blindness ideology, see Bonilla-Silva (2006, p. 3). See also Atwater (2008).
7. For more on the landmark case that legalized de jure racism, see Plessy v. Ferguson, 163 U. S. 537 (1896).
8. For more on the culture wars, see Banks (1996) and Hirsch (2001).

In the Field

In the last chapter, I discussed how race matters particularly in terms of education, and described the new aversive racism of color blindness as a postmodern factor in the schooling experiences and outcomes of students of color (Black and Latino males) through the theoretical lens of critical race theory. The discussion was informed by the argument that a student's race has a significant bearing on their educational outcomes, and that today racism is systemically and structurally institutionalized, creating barriers to achievement and future success. School systems present systemically prohibitive factors in climate; discipline policy and practice; zero tolerance policy; suspensions; overrepresentation in special education usage; and the level of cultural competence on the part of faculty, administration, and staff. These all contribute to students' poor relationships with their White teachers, as well as the low expectations many teachers hold of their students. These factors play an intrinsic role in academic achievement. Hence, the research clearly informs us of a variety of factors both inside and outside of the school that affect the educational outcomes for males of color, leading them to either disengage or stay engaged, creating for some, poor outcomes post graduation.

The concepts or domains outlined in the literature offer a framework for analysis as to how they may relate to as well as contribute to meaningful engagement and positive achievement outcomes. The domains relate to climate, in-the-school expectations of teachers and other adults, beliefs, impacts, and relationships that prohibit or enhance student achievement. Special education is not only a vehicle to label Black boys as defective, but it is the first doorway to harsh discipline practice and outcomes such as suspensions, expulsions, and dropping out.[1]

Vermont-centric research that has focused on Black males' public school experiences, have primarily been through the testimonial accounts of adults who have advocated on their students' behalf (Vermont Advisory Committee to the United States Commission on Civil Rights,

1999). Nevertheless, as noble as it may seem, no one, no matter how close, can tell another's story but the person disclosing. In fact, "most qualitative study seeks to understand and interpret how various participants in a specific social setting construct the world around them through the lens of the observer" (Glesne, 2006, p. 4). I am, however, very curious about how Black males themselves construct meaning from their schooling experiences as Black males in a majority White space. The sole role I play in this process is that of the messenger, nothing more.

Furthermore, I deeply believe that personal perspective is one of the most valuable means to bring lived experiences to the audience that needs to know, such as educational policy makers, stakeholders, and the educational community at-large. Primary voice can make a powerful and positive contribution in problem-solving social justice and equity issues and decision-making, contributing not only to positive experiences of future students, but also to the "lives of the participants themselves" (Glesne, 2006, p. 2). The young men who shared their perspectives have much to say about what life was like in school, but because of invisibility they have not had the opportunity or the venue to speak their truth to the powers that exist in the institution. The journey to finding their voice started with my deep commitment to social justice and equity. Finding those voices started with sharing my concern with anyone who was willing to listen in the greater community. Finding young men willing to share, was now my mission, no matter where I had to go to find them.

On the Road to Justice

Although the largest proportion of Vermont's African American population resides within Chittenden County, a broader range of perspectives was collected from across the state. Searching for individuals willing to share their perspectives was like searching for a needle in a haystack. Most people who know me well know my passion for equity, especially educational equity. Guided by a deep sense of justice, I spoke to just about anyone and everyone who would listen. Responses ranged from "Vermont is very liberal and we treat everyone the same here, we don't see race," to, "we don't have the populations here, so we don't have the dropout rates like in urban areas." I, however, would not be satisfied with those attempts to brush these important concerns aside, and was determined to look at the deeper question of what is really going on with Black young males in the public schools. Especially since we have a documented history in the schools and very little, if any, follow-up to the issues of race and equity. Can anyone really tell us what is going on? This is not rocket science, or is it? And it certainly is not a hunt for who is graduating and who is not. The research clearly states that poverty is not the only indicator of poor schooling experiences for Black males (Allen, 2010). We must look at race as well.

Perhaps, just considering the state's racial history, considering its place in the social order is enough to make one pause to think critically about the condition for students of color in our schools. The statistics and facts are right here, under our noses. Some of the data (Schott Foundation on Education, 2010) actually state that Black boys experience a higher percentage of being placed in special education classes as well as get disciplined more often than their White counterparts. So how can we, in any conscious mind, rationalize all of the data that point to issues with how young Black males experience their education in Vermont public school environments with outcomes that parallel the national data? And if they are graduating, what kind of life awaits them on the other side of graduation? Are they going off to college, or finding meaningful work? Have they been given the tools and skills they need in order to reach their highest potential? I have a sense of urgency while others seem to drag their feet on these very same issues. After much deliberation, many conversations, and false starts, trying to locate potential participants, I finally acquired some solid leads.

Trust Is the Key to Access and Entry

Because African Americans in Vermont make up a small percentage of the overall state population, I found it impossible to locate former students through any other means than by asking people if they knew of any Black males who attended public schools here. The first voice appeared through the networks in the community (both black and white) that knew men who were interested in sharing their perspectives (Wright & Decker, 1997). This lead emerged out of my conversations with many people at the community level. When a name came to my attention, I then contacted potential participants by cold call as well as e-mail for a chance to introduce the purpose and intention of my mission to them. After being clear in the right to share or not share and, at any time, if he wanted, to withdraw his voice, the participant agreed to be interviewed and we moved into the next phase of engagement. With genuine interest, willingness, and gratitude, the participant and I set up a time for an interview. Through this first contact, I was then able to connect and engage with others, through snowball sampling.

After numerous phone calls and a few failed attempts in catching up with busy young men, I finally arranged to meet a young man whom for the sake of anonymity, I will call Pete, somewhere in the state. Like Pete, all other participants have had their names as well as locations changed for the sake of protecting their privacy and anonymity.

Pete

It is a balmy, pre-fall day. The search to engage with Pete and his story has led me driving through a few seemingly quaint yet at times unquestionably impoverished sections of Vermont. Perhaps this drive was clearly a reminder of the myriad of factors that brought me here almost thirty-one years ago. Lucid memories carried with them a pleasant feeling, such as the kind one feels when one lives in scenic, green environments like Vermont, with its hamlets, small villages, and towns, its snowcapped mountains and rolling hills. Living habitats separated by what seemed to be endless, expansive farmlands.

I, too, wonder how Pete negotiated the terrain of race relations and the experience as "other" in this predominantly White sphere? What was his individual experience like? What analysis did his lens create for him?

Statistics tell us the state is a safe haven to educate and raise children, and that it is a child-friendly, thus family-friendly space. Factors that perhaps, might have brought this young man's family here, as it did me.

The data also tell us however, that people of color get profiled and stopped at a rate disproportionately higher to their White counterparts. Here in the state the data further inform us that African American males or Black males end up in the justice system at higher rates than their White counterparts (Justice Policy Institute, 2005).

The major conflict for me is the message of "safe" schools, but safe for whom? Especially when the data also tell us that males of color are graduating to the degree of an inverted gap, yet are affected by discipline and special education placement at higher rates then their White counterparts. After reviewing much of the data, I believe that we have to delve deeper, even beneath the surface.

Yes, it is great that males of color are graduating to the point of being off the charts. However, the test scores at pivotal points in their educations[2] are telling us that they are lagging behind their White counterparts in terms of math and reading. They are graduating, but for some they are unprepared by their marginal educations to lead meaningful, productive lives.

Nonetheless, driving through rural villages, towns, and hamlets lined with majestic, spreading shade maples on both sides of the street, I think about the possibilities of finally getting subjugated voices out to the public. I am drawn into the beauty of the drive, which has made me look forward to a conversation with a young man who was recommended by a friend of a friend of a friend. After two and a half hours on the road I finally reached my destination. A short drive from the center of town I approached a massive, antique, "red" house. A Vermont farmhouse with a white, fenced-in yard and what appeared to be pretty ancient fruit trees lining the long driveway stands out in a huge acreage of farmland. I parked in front of the barn. As I exited the car, I knew on a very instinctual level that I was on to a noble mission.

This house was not unusual by any means, except for its division into apartments for two households. Its enormity spoke to the previous souls who conversed in days past on the porches under the spreading maples. From the entrance, I saw a tattered relic of a volleyball net blowing in the breeze, as well as a set of bocce balls in stainless steel.

From the looks of the yard, and the well-tread grounds, this was a space where friendly or maybe not-so-friendly competition had routinely occurred. Evidence of vitamin water and beer cans verified that this was certainly a place where young adults gathered. My instincts and attention to detail were explicitly clear, informing the onlooker that young people reside here. There was a small, handmade sign with information for visitors as well as the sign on the front door with the occupants' name and message, "Come around the back and ring the bell please." So I refrained from knocking on the front door and followed the directive, leading me to the stairway up at the back of the house. Climbing the one flight of outdoor stairs, I come upon a back porch entry to the apartment I was seeking. In the stand of majestic shade maples a screened in porch to the right, draws me in. I would expect the occupants spend a lot of time out here. When I knocked on the door I was warmly received by a young man, somewhere between the ages of 19 and 24. After all the formalities of first introductions he asked me if I "would I like to sit inside or out on the porch?" It did not take much nor long to make up my mind, realizing that it is days like these that make us want to stretch summer into the early fall days like this very one. The splendor of the shade maples prompted me to accept the invitation to sit on a back porch. Sitting there in this small New England town offered quite a backdrop for sharing the story I was seeking. How comfortable to sit in this cozy yet exposed outdoors and ask a few questions about his school experiences.

I filled Pete in on the project and how verbal informed consent works. I also let him know that anytime he was interested in leaving the project he was free to do so, no questions asked. Pete confidently responded with, "I have nothing to hide, actually I'm very happy that someone's interested in what I think or have to say. I thought for the longest time no one actually cared."

Finally, I had access and entry. After offering me a cold beverage, which I thankfully accepted, I was ready to begin. Before we proceeded on with questions about what life was like for a Brown kid in a predominantly White school, I asked Pete to tell me a little about himself. He was open and very willing to share his story, and after mapping his life, the conversation became serious once we hit on the subject of school. School became the focus with which our discussions became grounded and intentional.

Pete came to Vermont when he was a toddler and had attended the Vermont public schools throughout to graduation. He moved here after trans-racial adoption. Even though he was raised in a loving home, he still had losses as a young boy that according to him "perpetually contributed to feelings of loss, misunderstanding, and confusion." It was not uncommon in the summer to be asked if he was a "Fresh Air" kid. That certainly did not help with his feeling of belonging. There were also cultural misunderstandings that often impacted his schooling interactions with both peers and adults. Early on he developed a clear realization that race was central to some of the dynamics of engagement within his journey through school and the world.

After filling me in on his bio I proceeded to ask, "Please describe what elementary and middle school were like for you?" Pete sipped his beverage thoughtfully, deeply, pondering the question put before him. He talked about growing up in isolation, being surrounded by people, yet feeling alone in a sea of homogeneity. It did not take long for him to come to the realization that he was the factor of difference, whenever and wherever he entered. His story talked about the teachers that did not know what to make of him, and the resulting confusion that caused him to act out and resist their conflicts on some occasions, especially when it seemed to be related to moments of a cultural disconnection between a Brown boy's way of being, in a sea of preconceived notions about who he was and who he was expected to be. That sea was a sea of Whiteness. He spoke of his observations in his experience in a public school system where the teachers not only did not look like him, but also held preconceived notions about him—notions, according to him, that focused on his behavior and capacity. He spent a large portion of his education in the planning room.

We talked for what seemed like hours, but in reality within the span of an hour's time Pete conversed further about his dreams, his aspirations and social dynamics, as well as his journey from kindergarten to 12th grade in systems that did not really know what to make of or how to relate to him. His numerous experiences spending time in the planning room in the early days of his schooling, and the out-of-school suspension he experienced in high school, impacted his relationships and participation in class activities for his culminating year. Pete concluded by offering some really good advice about how he saw school in meeting the needs of students who are non-White. Pete seemed very animated when he shared the course of his life. There is a philosophical dimension—a quality of his personality and demeanor. Meeting with Pete made me very hopeful. I was hopeful in the sense that he was very open and transparent about his perceptions and views on school. He was very clear about feelings of isolation and misunderstanding. Over the course of his schooling, he had spent much time in the planning room over solvable issues. I admire his willingness to refer others to the project. I believe it means that on some level he trusts the intentions behind this mission. Perhaps he realizes that his voice does count, even many years later. Pete now lives on his own, after traveling and living outside of the state for a few years, just after graduation.

Pete has been back in the area for a little over a year. He shares an apartment with a few mates, and is working.

After thanking Pete, I reminded him that at any time, if he wanted to retract his voice from the project, he was free to do so. No obligation, no questions asked. I then moved on to the task of asking him about any other young men he knew who might be interested. Pete told me about George, a friend who went to school with him but whose family moved and is now living in another part of the state. With baseline information and a few leads in hand, the snowball effect was in progress. The next step in my journey was to find George and his perspective to add to this mission for educational justice.

George

After a series of confirming dates and times via email correspondence, George finally agreed to meet me at a local coffee shop on the outskirts of a neighboring town. It is a slightly overcast day, one of three days in which we have endured what appears to be too much rain. Rivers and streams are on the edge of cresting. Rain has been coming down in intermittent downpours as I set off to find a small watering hole that is welcoming, warm, and somewhat quiet.

Arriving at my destination with a few minutes to spare, I find myself between the café entrance and an ensuing sprinkle. The only thing between us is my age and lack of ability to sprint like the days of my youth. Age aside, needing to protect my gear, I rapidly find my way to the entrance of this homey café in search of refuge as well as sanctuary from the impending storm not too far off in the distance.

Once inside I scan the place for a semi-private space in order to speak with George. I stake my claim on an arrangement of three large, cushy chairs at the back of the café, set down my belongings, and head towards the front of the café for a hot cup of tea. Walking to place my order, I noticed outside the window, a threatening cloud coverage rolling in from the west, which appeared to spread a somewhat mysteri-ous and unpredictable shroud over the landscape.

Nevertheless, I enjoyed the momentary streaks of intense light peering through the cloud veils.

I enter the café amidst the sound of music and the smell of freshly roasted coffee rhythmically grinding in the background. The atmosphere is somewhat low-key and very laid back, Vermont style. The music is playing softly in the background—a very familiar reggae classic, a Bob Marley tune, "Jammin"—which, on this somewhat cool, wet day takes me momentarily into my imagination to places far from Vermont's ever-changing and unpredictable, stormy climate.

The music seems to have set the tone for both the house staff and its patrons, in the fragrant and slowly filling room. From Bob Marley to Crosby, Stills, Nash, and Young, now playing, I take delight in the selection thus far. I snuggle into a comfy, overstuffed chair and claim my station, a seat in the window, where I can keep my eye on both worlds. It is 1:50 in the afternoon. I have noticed that not more than ten minutes has passed, and the seating area is thinning, when all of a sudden a sizable group of women invades the place nonstop trying to beat the rain that is now on the heels of their shiny, rubber rain boots. There are four people seated along the window already as well. However, just as quickly as the seating area is filled, it is emptied. Within the frame of ten minutes the café becomes less active. And the colorful, rainboot-clad women are back outside to tread through the downpour.

Now I have the area to myself again. This lull in time and space gives me a chance to reflect on why this work project is important not only to me, but also to others who do this work. I am always asking myself, "Where is the urgency?" Especially since folks are asking what is going on? Am I being an alarmist? I don't know. What I do know is that the data tell me, however, that some thing is not right, even if males are graduating. How many of them had expectations for a meaningful future, or were directed and educated for a place in the academy? Did they take honors or AP classes? Did their teachers tell them that they could achieve whatever they wanted to? Was the environment of the school itself safe for them to be their authentic selves? Did they have teachers who cared and saw all of their potential in a positive light?

I am just curious, and this curiosity has really driven my mission to get to the bottom of this elusive issue. One thing for sure, when I talk to some folks about these issues they genuinely understand where I am coming from. As well they should. Often our shared sense of urgency has not put us in the greatest of grace with some in powerful positions in the institutions.

Nonetheless, I will not give up the struggle to get to the bottom of this dilemma. Because in the long run all of our futures depend on it. This may be an important moment. I can only hope. I am worrying a little. It is now fifteen minutes past two. Did George have second thoughts about revealing his schooling past to a stranger?

I will give it another 15 minutes. I hope my curiosity about the experiences of young males of color does not open up a can of worms for them. Even if they had good experiences in their own perceptions, and even if they are graduates, their stories are important and need to be heard. Moreover, change cannot be made to better the circumstances for all students if we do not tap into the wisdom of those who have already made it through the gauntlet.

Just the other day I was dialoging with the parent of a former local public school graduate, who shared not only her frustrations with public schools here but also the frustrations her son holds for his marginal education. He was one of many who graduated with the reading level of a sixth grader and a fifth-grade math level. This form of graduation by social promotion only produces marginal life outcomes. Students meet the minimal requirements to pass the classes, thus accrue the grades in order to graduate. They are marginal because they graduate meeting minimal expectations, nearly at the bottom of the class. I really feel her outrage because I have heard about this issue from others as well. A few more minutes and I will have to depart this neck of the woods. Is this opportunity missed, or maybe it is just not the right time or place now? As I begin to gather up my tools of the trade for interviewing, the door opens and a young male of color between the ages of twenty and twenty-five walks in with two small children in tow. He looks as though he is looking for someone. I wave and smile, not wanting to appear assuming. He acknowledges with a smile, and comes over with his small charges. George and I are now formally introduced. He also introduced his little companions, twins Tristan and Baker.

He apologizes for being late and explains the two young ones accompanying him. The twins happen to be one of his many obligations on his day off from school and work. He takes care of his niece and nephew, while his sister, a single mom works. He asks the children what they want to drink and together the three head for the coffee bar. They return within a few minutes with a tall cup of iced coffee and each of the two children carrying their own beverages. He takes one of the two fluffy seats left across from me after settling the children in on the other with a small corner table on which to place their drinks. Taking books from his backpack, he lovingly sets them on task and proceeds to give me his undivided attention.

I begin the conversation by explaining to George the purpose and reasoning behind this project, and that I really appreciated his going out of his way to make time so he could lend his voice to the unrecognized voices hidden in the shadows of the Green Mountains. To that he added "invisible." After all of the formalities we get to the task at hand, the interview. I asked George to tell me a little bit about himself and then proceeded to ask him the first of twelve key questions, starting with "Please describe what elementary school was like for you." Before answering the first question George told me a little about himself.

His close-knit family moved here from the West when he was in the third grade. He had attended two Vermont public schools since the third grade, with his last move placing him in a district from the sixth grade through graduation. His family moved here when he was eight years old because they wanted a change from the West Coast and had heard that Vermont was a good place to raise children and had better schools for both him and his older sister. They moved to Vermont in search of fulfilling that dream. I asked him to describe what it was like for him in both elementary and middle school.

Although George was an above-average student, he felt very invisible and often experienced little attention and encouragement from his teachers. In high school he felt he was just in the background, and if it was not for his family he might have had bigger challenges. He took school seriously, yet felt he did not get the assistance he needed to get into a good college after high school. In hindsight, he felt as though he was not directed to the right classes that would help a student get into college. George recounted few friendships in both elementary and high school. Sports did not interest him at all. Art and music were his passions.

However, by middle school he really never had a good friend with whom he could be himself, much less rely on. Throughout middle and high school he had less than a handful of folks he would consider friends today. Most were acquaintances or folks he saw in the halls. On many occasions he had to deal with racial bullying on the bus with name calling particularly the N-word.

He was an oddity in a sense, because as he put it, he was not the stereotype many perceived him to be. George attributes it to the fact that he is somewhat quiet and also did not buy into the whole gangster, hip-hop look that many White males up here in Vermont subscribe to. He got tired of explaining to people that not every Black person is into hip-hop, and even if they are into the music, it does not mean they are into the fashion. That mind-set also went with sports. George was never an athlete, nor did he aspire to be. Yet he was constantly asked if he would like to play basketball. He further explained that he found joy in drawing, music, and other artistic pursuits. He wished that people did not pigeonhole him. He wished they understood that buying into stereotypes will not help matters if you do not know about people. He feels that people should not try so hard, that they should relax and get to know people by first seeing and acknowledging them. See them as human beings who want the same things and dream the same dreams as White students.

At the end of our conversation I informed George that if he wanted to leave the project he was free to do so at any time, no questions asked.

With a final handshake and a thank you, I asked George one last question: Did he know of any other young men of color who went to school here and who might be interested in having me capture their story? With not much to go on as far as offering possible voices, I thanked George for his time and perspectives.

George is a serious and responsible young man, who spent his early youth growing up in Vermont, attending public schools from elementary through high school. His openness and willingness to share his story are in hopes of influencing policy for future students in public schools. Meeting with George enlightened me, opening my eyes to the level of isolation and cultural misunderstanding that males of color, or students who are perceived as different, can experience if they are the only student (or one of a few students) of a different race in a majority White school. Since graduating from high school, George is working.

Malcolm

I was beginning to worry. A week and a half had passed. Not hearing from anyone or having much luck with leads concerned me. Then Malcolm called, out of the blue. He said he learned from a friend that there was a woman looking to talk to males of color who went to public school in Vermont. He stated enthusiastically that he wanted to speak of his experiences and that he had some perspectives worth sharing. I was really curious about what he had to say. I knew of incidents in the schools that involved males of color that could be considered common in today's school environment. Moreover, I myself personally have witnessed some really unconscious behavior associated with cultural and systemic norms in some schools across the state. For example, in my observations, in some schools they hold an event between grades called "master-servant day." I was so taken by this as a social event in a public school that I began to ask about its history. I was told that in some Vermont schools "slave" day was also a norm. What we have here is a perfect example of cultural incompetence. An event planned with good intentions, I am sure, without considering from a socioeconomic perspective how offensive that might be to people marginalized by social class.

Nonetheless, Malcolm's response really got my adrenaline going. I was curious and excited to meet him and hear what he had to say. He met me at his current home a few miles from where he originally grew up. With time to spare between his full-time job and school, we sat and talked before he had to leave for work. Like the young men preceding him, I asked Malcolm to tell me a little bit about himself before we got into the interview questions.

Malcolm moved to Vermont with his mother, a single parent from a large city, during first grade. She, who was both divorced and a nurse, had always expected her only child to take school seriously. Therefore, she required that he make school and his school work a priority before all other things. He said his mother had hopeful dreams for him. The move here was not only a big sacrifice financially and socially, but he realized that the move was about his having the opportunity to have a better life than what they had left behind in the city. I then asked him to describe what elementary and middle school was like for him.

When it came time to get down to the business of schooling stories, Malcolm talked about first grade and his view of the reality of difference and how it was handled in the schools from an early age. He further disclosed numerous incidents where stereotypical racial insults from his peers were a common, almost daily occurrence, and the indifference of some of his teachers in responding to the hurtful bullying and harassment. Malcolm, in his mature demeanor, chalked it all up to personal ignorance. His explanation was that "parents teach the child." These occurrences happened more regularly starting in middle school, continuing into high school as well.

Another thing that Malcolm made clear was that he did not see much of himself in the curriculum, and he grew up with the normative heroes used by schools to engage students through the holiday framework—the traditional stories of Rosa Parks and the civil rights movement, players we all know about. Malcolm, however, wanted to hear and learn more stories about those who were not at the forefront of the movement. His grandparents were involved in voter registration in the sixties. He talked about how they were on the bus and they sat down at lunch counters. They marched for social justice. They fought for the right to vote. And then to move here, knowing that they sacrificed because they were interested in him having a decent education. The schools, in his eyes, were not meeting those needs for him.

Nonetheless, that did not get in the way for him. Unfortunately, he did not have an opportunity to have any teachers that looked like himself in his classes. Along the way he did have a teacher that seemed to be interested in him and what he thought and found important in middle school. His recollections of a teacher who noticed his interest in the history of Black people was truly what had sustained him and kept him engaged in school. Our deep conversations made us lose track of time. Malcolm needed to leave for work. I thanked him for his candidness and asked him if he knew of any other young men like himself who might be also interested.

Malcolm's experiences brought to light the level of covert bullying and harassment that can impact students of color in the school setting, along with the covert style of cloaked stereotype threats that at times interfered with his ability to learn and thrive in school.

Malcolm's experiences were also affected by his acute awareness that something was missing from the curriculum.

Damon

All I can say is "What perfect timing!" On the heels of my last interview, Damon agrees to meet and discuss his schooling. The eatery where I met Damon was just emptying out from the lunchtime rush. I was worried about finding a space that was both quiet and unobtrusive. It was a major concern because I wanted to make sure Damon was comfortable speaking his truth.

Setting down the small, steaming pot of vanilla chai, like clockwork, I prepared myself for the meeting I had scheduled with him a few days earlier. According to my watch, Damon was right on schedule. He was youthfully upbeat and energetic. With time passing, I went over the terms of the verbal consent and proceeded to ask Damon about himself before moving on to the interview questions. According to Damon, he grew up in a single-parent household with his mom and older brother. Damon was a good student and school seemed to be uneventful until the end of one of his elementary years, when he had a teacher who was obviously inattentive and disinterested in getting to know him or to put any time or effort into his needs in the classroom. Being the "only" student of color within this classroom, Damon felt invisible. He was not invisible to his peers in terms of occasional bullying and harassment, however, but invisible to the teacher. That year was very frustrating, so Damon spent the next year being homeschooled. He loved homeschooling, but felt it was impractical in terms of the social life that extracurricular activities offered him by being on the school campus.

By the time he went to the public high school, however, he had to negotiate what he described as the larger jungle of assumptions, gossip, and mean-spiritedness perpetrated by both students and teachers alike—assumptions filled with stereotypes and backed up by microaggressions. He experienced a few incidents where racial language played into the equation. Assumptions by some of his peers were laced with descriptors defining him by societal norms. The overall climate, filled with teenage angst and exclusion, also deeply bothered him. The lack of positive Black male role models was frustrating as well. He named one teacher, however, who saw his gift for writing and invited him to take an honor English class. However, it was his tenacity and deep sense of self, along with both familial expectations and support, that helped him find his way to both graduation and the possibilities of college.

A scholarly young man, Damon talked about being out of school now for a little over a year. He expressed concern about the depressed economy and finding funding to go to college. He is looking into going to community college at the moment because it seems to be the only option he may have now. Furthermore, he is also planning on going to community college because he feels that school fell short on what he needed to do to get into a university. His future designs hold the hope of going to a mainstream university. The state of the economy and the feeling of not being adequately prepared for college due to the misguidance of those charged with directing students toward postsecondary education were deep disappointments to him. In his senior year, however, he figured out that he did not get what he needed from school in order to achieve his goals. "I picked up the pieces and made do with what I got out of high school," he clearly stated. Meanwhile, not letting that hold him back, he has enrolled in community college and plans to matriculate to the university. For now, that is his game plan.

Damon attended Vermont public schools all through his primary and secondary educational career, except for a year off when he was being homeschooled. He is now attending college in hopes of becoming an English teacher. He is bright and interested in intellectual pursuits. He is looking forward to becoming an English major because it is a subject that he excelled in during high school. The question I ask is, "If he took an advanced placement English class, how come no one in school guided him toward college?"

Noel

It feels good to be back on familiar turf. Do not get me wrong: all the driving across this beautiful state proved to be well worth it, not only for my soul, but also for my mind. However, this story-seeking jaunt into town made the intensity of this project somewhat joyous and hope-filled on this cool, rainy day in August. After looking for parking close to the campus, I rushed across the green in order to meet up with my next storyteller. Noel agreed to meet me at a popular café on the university campus.

Meeting him served two purposes. One, to find a quiet space to talk and interview just before the onslaught of students ready to take over town for the new semester, and two, for Noel to do some shopping for school downtown, before he sets out on his second year as a nontraditional student at a local technical college. We seemed to coordinate this meeting intuitively. For him, the campus café presented the opportunity to pick up some things at the bookstore. I was very thankful that he was willing to go out of his way to share his experiences through the halls of Vermont's public schools.

As I am sitting here in this student-centered building, sipping a warm, spiced beverage, I am thinking (actually having second thoughts), going over the same question in my head multiple times, "Is this an appropriate place to meet?" Of course it is. This space was his suggestion to begin with. Furthermore, one thing that we can do is decide upon his arrival where we can find another space to interview if need be. In this choice I defer to Noel and what would be comfortable and safe for him.

It is about 11:30 a.m. and Noel should be arriving at any moment. As usual, I neurotically checked and rechecked to make sure that my recording device was charged and ready to function. The last thing I want at this juncture is device failure. By the time I finished taking inventory of the tools on my interview checklist, Noel had arrived. Smiling courteously, he extended his hand to shake mine and proceeded to take a seat in the chair to my left, just in front of the fireplace. I ask if he feels comfortable sitting here and mention that if he does not, we can find another, more comfortable, private space somewhere else. He quickly scans the scene and agrees to stay put. After going over the project, and, of course, his participation in it, I ask Noel to just fill me in a bit about his life.

Noel proceeds to inform me that his family arrived in Vermont before he was born. His family at the time consisted of his dad, mom, and two older siblings. They were committed to two things: the search for a better, safer place to raise their children, and the ability to find work opportunities in the service sector. They ended up living outside a former industrial mill town, on the outskirts of a small, rural community.

After the brief yet intriguing bio, I proceeded to ask Noel, "What was elementary and middle school like?" He replied, "From the first grade I noticed a lot of politeness from my teachers." Furthermore, the politeness did not feel at all genuine. It seemed as though they were afraid of him. Mind you, from my observations there is nothing intimidating about this young man. In the classrooms, teachers very rarely called on him even when he raised his hand for an answer. He was not really encouraged to speak out in the classroom unless he was asked occasionally to represent the viewpoint of his perceived racial affiliation. Most of the classes he took were vocational or tech courses. He found school boring. His saving grace was computers. Everybody thought he should play sports, for which he had no interest or ability, due to his asthma. Jokingly, he stated, "I might have considered it if I had attended a school with a pool and a swim team." High school was pretty uneventful for Noel. With few (if any) friends, and classes that never really sparked his passions and interested him, Noel drifted through school. After graduation, he took a computer tech class. He wondered why no one directed him to computer classes at school. He has been working with computers ever since and decided to go to college and learn more about the field of computer technology and graphic design.

Noel attended public schools through to high school graduation. Growing up in Vermont, he was well aware of the diversity. He says both students and teachers alike through their attitudes quite often reminded him about race. He now works and is attending school part-time for his degree in computer sciences. Noel is married and is the father of three children.

Roger

Today I am heading south to meet up with Roger at a nearby park on Lake Champlain. Roger was very gracious to meet me there. Forty-five minutes in the car and I reach my destination. What better place to meet than at one of my favorite historic sites in the state, Lake Champlain Maritime Museum. At this time of year the population has dwindled to a trickle. Not much action other than busloads of school children and the few tourists passing through to admire one of the state's national treasures. It is leaf-peeping season, signaling tourists from all over.

There are plenty of places to sit to take in the beauty, and listen to stories.

The breathtaking beauty of the maples in their full fall splendor, with colors and trees etched not only with webs of color but with a deep sense of history as well. A variety of outlooks here in this place speaks to many stories told and untold through the eyes of both the victor and the vanquished. A plethora of subjugated stories, many hidden, some not, in the deep recesses of those who breathed the air and walked the lands, long before we arrived at this time. What are the stories of those who lived and still live in the shadows of the green mountains? The people of the dawn land who had to endure the journey with two feet straddling two worlds. What did they say as they sat among the maples, discoursing about their hopes for the future yet unborn?

As I pulled in to the agreed destination, I found the reference marker, all the while being consumed by the spectacular colors on this crisp day. I followed a winding path, leading me to where I needed to park my car in the parking lot. I eventually located a parking space and met Roger who had been, in his own words, "waiting just under a minute." We set out to seek a quiet space to sit, finally finding a picnic table facing the lake. After verbally agreeing to the informed consent I put before him, I asked Roger to fill me in on his story.

Roger's family hails from the northeastern part of the state, just on the Canadian border. He, however, was born a little more than twenty-five years ago out of state while his folks were in the military, where they both met. The family moved to and settled in a different part of the state when he was four. Roger has attended public school since then, and from the age of twelve attended middle school all the way through high school.

Roger begins by talking about his dad's side of the family and growing up in a family of Vermonters who had moved here, during the Back-to-the-land movement of the early 1960s, and how they set down their roots. He said that his grandparents were folks who moved here because they wanted to live where the environment was conducive for getting in touch with nature and the land. They were both retired activists, who moved here after living on a commune elsewhere in New England. Roger's dad also attended school in majority White, predominantly rural areas and came back for just that reason: to have access to land that would produce a big garden for the family to put up for the winter. They somehow made it work. By farming, working and raising families, they prospered. Roger's father joined the military after graduating from high school and was sent off to Georgia, where he met Roger's mother. They got married and had Roger, their only son. They moved to Vermont when he was four, and this is where he has been ever since. He has family on his mother's side in Virginia.

He felt that he did not notice or have problems personally with anyone. Roger talked about what it was like to be in the classroom as well as the hallways where bullying and harassment often missed the eyes of adults. He believed it was "more ignorance than race, though" that drove these occurrences. By the time he was in high school he went to class and did not bother anyone. He found that no one bothered him either. He worked hard at remaining invisible. A self-described introvert, he did not make fast friends, even though he got along with everyone. As he put it, he minded his business and stayed out of trouble. The extent of his high school experiences was that he went to school, did the work, and went home and listened to music. Our conversation was enlightening and very informative.

Afterwards, I reassured Roger that anytime he wanted to retract his perspective he was free to do so, with no questions asked. He also offered me some leads to follow but could not assure me that the persons would be interested or that the leads would amount to anything. He really did not know many Black people except for his mother's family, all of who lived in Virginia.

Roger was born outside the state while his parents were in the military. His father is a native born Vermonter and his mother hails from Virginia. After their military service they came to Vermont to raise Roger and his younger sister. Roger attended Vermont public schools from kindergarten through graduation and is now working.

Warwick

I have been to many malls in my life. To be honest, they are my least favorite places on the planet. If I have to shop, I love shopping local. But for malls it is the whole commercial atmosphere of capitalism at its height that is troubling for me. Over the years I have developed a deep dislike for malls. However, for the sake of capturing the story, the social observer must go to places that might be uncomfortable for them if these places are comfortable physically and emotionally for the participant.

I am by no means a curmudgeon on malls and the joy they bring to some folks. It is just that malls have always creeped me out. I do not know if it is because of the incident when my daughter was very young and a creepy man tried to lure her away from me, right before my eyes, or whether it is about being in what I see as the den of capitalist greed? Perhaps, it is the drive to spend in this consumer culture that we have all inherited? I don't really know. Nonetheless, I am not that fond of malls, but will go for the sake of authentic research.

I met with Warwick just after his evening shift ended, where he works as a retail manager. Warwick offered to meet me at the food court. Right near the pizza vendor. On the phone he expressed that he was interested in knowing more about the project and its purpose, but was leery as to why folks would want to hear from him. What does he have to say that will make a difference? What I found most intriguing in his questioning was his need to understand how his participation would make a difference. He seemed a little skeptical at first, but after I explained the project's purpose he was fully on board. After bringing him up-to-date on protocol and gaining his verbal consent, I asked him to tell me a little about himself.

Warwick came to Vermont with his mother and two younger sisters from a large, urban school district in another state during the middle of fourth grade. He graduated from a local Vermont high school. Warwick told his story of growing up in a single-parent household here in Vermont, although that is not how his life here in the United States started off. As Warwick explained, his mother followed his father to the US from Guyana when he was three years old. Prior to moving to Vermont, they all lived in an urban area, and he attended an inner city school until the fourth grade, just after his parents divorced. Warwick's mother headed north, in search of new beginning following her divorce.

He shared his shock of moving to Vermont at the age of ten, going into public schools that, in comparison to the ones he attended in his former community, were at least peaceful. He did not have to worry about the kind of violence that was commonplace prior to his arrival here. His mother was strict and expected him to listen in school and do his work. She said that school took priority over all other things except work. Because his mother was a single parent he was expected to work for the things beyond the basics as well as contribute to the house. I then asked him, "What were elementary and middle school like for you?" He noticed that some kids and teachers were what he perceived to be mean-spirited and racist toward him and others like him. Some days he was faced with racial epithets and bullying. Other days it was like he was invisible. This made it hard for him to feel included. At one point in his elementary school career he found himself the center of bullying and harassment and was often called a derogatory term. He carried the burden of bullying because of his fear of no one doing anything as well as retaliation. We then went on to the rest of the questions that I had everyone consider in their talks with me.

Warwick attended Vermont public schools since the age of ten. He moved here from a large, urban school district, was raised in a single-parent household, and holds a retail management job since graduating from high school

Luis

This journey today, after many days spent trying to locate more voices, is a very welcome one, to say the least. The drive is exceptional. It is obvious that the days of summer are moving rapidly along. I see a hint of color tucked in some groves of standing trees along the western ridge-line of the hills. I am overjoyed that for some reason this process, although time consuming, has been producing some very enlightening responses.

Finally getting a commitment from Luis was a long-awaited accom-plishment. His willingness was a very pleasant surprise. As with some of the other young men, it was hard to pinpoint a date, much less schedule time to talk. I knew it was not because of some fear of sharing their stories' but because these young men lead very busy lives.

These winding, long country roads led me to Luis. I met up with him at his house in a small, rural, mountain community. After a short ride across the state we met to find out just what his views on Vermont public schools might be. I made it very clear to Luis that he was in no way obligated to disclose, or to be part of the project. He had only to let me know and I would retract his comments, no questions asked. He liked that and then wholeheartedly agreed to participate. After telling him my purpose for the project I proceeded to ask him to tell me a bit about himself before we went on to the twelve questions I had prepared.

Luis was quite animated as he talked about his Vermont family on his mom's side. They took great pride in being multigenerational Vermonters, none of who had ever gone to college. They were farmers, land-rich but dirt-poor. His dad and mom divorced when he was two years old. His dad, now remarried with a new family, took pride in hailing from Philly.

He was both frank and honest about his experiences. Being the son of an urban Black man and growing up in the "outback" (his term for rural, country, and farmland) was both good and bad. One of his passions was basketball. He did, however, express his dreams to go on to college, maybe even play a sport. He talked critically about his experiences in school, experiences with students and educators alike. He went on about coaches and teammates who insisted on using him during sports season, but never "had his back" when race issues showed up at games or out of the view of others. It appeared that for peers and some teachers there were only two possible categories in which Luis could be placed. One, they seemed to want to pigeonhole him as an athlete. Or two, some even thought he was the resident expert on Black culture. Like hip-hop and Gangster rap music. He found this troubling.

During his last year of school he got into two fights, ending up in suspension. The final straw for this college hopeful was a fight with another student who used a racial slur. The consequences were unequal and unjust. His justice? Suspension. For the other student, there were no consequences at all. At that point in his education Luis had finally had enough. He dropped out, got his GED, and now works in the family business as a mechanic. Today he regrets not finishing school with his class or going on to college, but feels he is okay doing the work he does. As Luis would say, "It's honest work." Time passed just as quickly as it had arrived. I assured Luis of his participation being fully voluntary and reminded him that if he wanted to retract his participation he was free to do so at any time. The ride home with plenty of transcribing and coding still to be accomplished, made me think of all the men I had interviewed to date. They all seemed to have very different yet similar experiences.

Luis attended public school during the secondary years. He ended his secondary education with more time in suspension, leading to his finally being forced to spend his senior year in an out-of-school suspension. He dropped out, got his GED and is now working.

Jason

Jason was in town on a visit to see his brother, and agreed to meet me at one of my favorite tea spots on the main drag. The arrangement worked out rather well and convenient for me after a day of meetings and advocacy work. Meeting with Jason was a refreshing reminder as to why I do the work that I do. The walk down from the hill over to Main Street gave me enough room between meetings to clear my head, to think about the stories I had heard up until now, and to ponder just what Jason might have to add to the narrative created by all the other voices before him.

Today this tea spot is barely full. There is something about this bohemian coffee spot that warms my heart and awakens my memory to the many cold days I spent studying with a spicy cup of hot, steamy ginger lemonade. This is a pretty popular local watering hole for the early morning crowd, as well as for those who may find its placement an advantage, next to one of the city's most notorious nightspots. This place had been one of my favored writing refuges while moving through my doctoral work at the University.

In a quiet space in the café Jason was sitting as if he was waiting to meet someone. I went up to him and introduced myself. After a brief introduction and articulating the purpose of the project, I asked Jason to tell me about himself. Jason talked about what brought him to Vermont. As a trans-racial adoptee, Jason grew up, was educated, and felt isolated in a predominantly White sphere. This story is very compelling and interesting, yet not unusual here in the North Country. Jason was adopted along with his younger brother by a White couple, and had attended Vermont public schools throughout his entire educational career. According to Jason his schooling experiences address climate, curriculum, and adults in the school who he felt "had his back." He did not realize he was different until someone pointed it out as a young child. Most of the incidents he experienced in school were related to comments people made that could be considered stereotype threats, such as comments about ability and skin color.

Jason talked about curriculum in his ninth-grade English classroom with a reading in which his class read some highly charged literature. When I asked him if he wanted to talk further about it he went into a description of all the things that can go wrong in a class where there is charged language, no preparation, and concrete thinking adolescents. Being the only Black face in the classroom made him very uncomfortable with having to be the focus of the discussion at times. Having a teacher who was delivering pretty complex reading materials, particularly with the use of the N-word, was a very clear warning. The word and its potential to create real havoc and chaos made him take action and talk to the school administrators.

Jason went on to say that the most important thing that he learned was that it is hard when you are dealing with a book with such racialized language and you have only one Black student in the classroom. Dealing with unwanted attention around race was problematic for him. So was race-based bullying and harassment.

In dealing with that word outside of the classroom he recalled a couple of incidences where there was graffiti written or verbal usage of the word. Once again, he felt very fortunate that he had relationships with administrators who attended to his concerns caringly and compassionately. That made high school tolerable. He had an adult who would have gone the extra mile to advocate on his behalf, even with teachers. This made all the difference in the world for him. There was some good in these relationships that he had throughout his career. There may not have been many, but they were strategic in helping him to negotiate the oftentimes-hostile climate of his high school.

Jason also had much to say about his parents, who opened up his world, enabling him to build on his own inner resilience to make his way through the starts and stops in environments where students can be very abusive to one another. Jason also talked about a couple of potential confrontations with students. He refused to engage with them, even when they tried to be physically abusive towards him. Fighting never resulted because he was always able to talk his way out or find the supports within the school to help him get through the situation.

Jason is currently employed, living and attending school out of state and starting a family. I thanked Jason for his time and story. As I started my car for the journey home I was amazed at the maturity and resilience that many of the young men in this project possess. Considering their stories, they are some of the most incredibly tenacious and resourceful men I have met in a very long time. Jason attended school throughout his education in Vermont and lives out of state. He is currently employed, and is raising a family.

Bill

I met Bill at a social gathering. We introduced ourselves. At first I thought he was originally from out of town due to the fact that he mentioned he lived someplace other than Vermont. I had been in a conversation with him about school and the work I do as well as asking him what factors brought him to Vermont for this occasion. He said he grew up here, just moved back, and knew the party host. I then asked him if he attended school here. The rest is classic. I asked if he was interested in sharing his insight. We agreed to create space and time prior to his departure to talk about his experiences with being schooled here in Vermont.

We set a time to meet before he headed out of town for vacation in the next few days. Catching up with Bill in the next few days turned into a few weeks. A few weeks was better than nothing, so I met him and we resumed our conversation about life in school in Vermont. I steered the conversation directly toward the purpose of the project, asking him to tell me about himself before I delved into the rest of the questions. According to Bill, for as long as he could remember, he had always wanted to live in Burlington. To him, it seemed much cooler and hipper, than the regions outside the city limits. That was not always the case though. He grew up in a small Vermont hamlet attending public schools until graduation. Both of his parents were entrepreneurs and were either traveling or busy working from their home office. Bill spoke of his experience of being an (if not the only) African American in his school. His elementary years were what he referred to as relatively non-descript. He did not seem to have too many intense brushes with students, except for what he called the usual boyish stuff. Bill talked about his experiences with bullying and harassment in middle school, describing too many brushes with teachers who were always ready to put him in the planning room. The biggest concern and issue he brought up was the lack of response from teachers when it came to students that were very unkind and basically showing very ignorant behavior or being racist. A couple of incidents he talked about made it very clear that there seemed to be a lack of care in his school. In one incident, a student said something derogatory and no one responded. Another incident occurred out of what seemed to be a misunderstanding between him and another student who made racially based comments about him. He suffered the consequences and was sent to in-school suspension. He started to wonder if there was something about him. He talked about those types incident having occurred on a couple of occasions in his educational career. What really turned him off was the notion of the planning room, which, in middle school, seemed to be reserved for the poor White and Brown boys. In high school he noticed that access to opportunities for enrichment was never put on the table. His parents would always ask why that was not the case for him. He had his parents advocate and challenge the system to get him into a class. Even with the grades he had they always tried to steer him away from those classes. He finally had a teacher who advocated for him by recommending him for honors classes.

After high school, Bill moved out of state for a while and is now back, working a full-time job. I thanked Bill for his time and valuable input into the project. I reminded him of his freedom to withdraw at any time, and told him I would be in touch for member checking.

Jermaine

Jermaine met me at the library. He had heard about the project from a long-time friend, Bill. They became fast friends in their youth, living out in the boondocks. After a year together in middle school they ended up going on to different high schools, completing their journey in different locations. His journey was the family move to the northeast, where he completed his education in isolation, with few friends like himself.

Jermaine talked not only about living in such an isolated place but also about the hardships of being Black in a place where you stand out and where you are feared. Living in a small town in a single-family household headed by a White mother in poverty had its impact on how he was received and perceived. Learning to negotiate the stereotypes that go along with that, Jermaine found that middle school was when the real challenges began for him. He acknowledges his mother's hard work and sacrifice so that her children could have a better life. He realizes that moving here from a rural area in another part of the state did not change much for her economically.

Bill attended Vermont public schools from elementary school to high school and is now working a full-time job. His issues were around school climate. School and home life had their ups and downs for Jermaine. He managed it all the best he could. Racial hate also permeated the environment, occasionally showing up on walls and sidewalks throughout the community. One incident that really "rocked his world" was when a cross was put on the lawn of someone in the community. He found that quite disturbing, and it made him and others fearful.

In high school there was one incident that he found odd, yet he chalked it up to the ignorance of the teacher. It was during a Civil War unit. He and another student of color were actually asked to stand in front of the classroom and sing the song "Dixie." At this point, you could hear the long pause between sentences. I think we both had to take a moment to breathe and reflect on what the teacher's motivation behind that act might have been. One could only imagine.

I thanked Jermaine, reminding him of our verbal consent and the option to drop out at any time. I had a lot to think about after the "Dixie" incident. The drive home gave me time to think about the food for thought to which I had just become privy.

Jermaine attended Vermont public schools since the elementary level and is currently employed and living in Vermont.

David

David and his family moved here from another part of the country when he was an infant. After David's mother died in childbirth, his father remarried a woman with two children a few years older than David. The couple decided to bring their newly blended family to Vermont. They arrived in time for David to start kindergarten. They moved to a small town where he and his siblings were enrolled in the local schools.

David did not really complain much about his experience. Having older siblings that had already made a way for him in school (all the way up to high school) seemed to be a helpful factor. It seemed to be easier for him, and I say that because he had older siblings that had gone to high school, were relatively good students, and did not create any problems.

They did have to negotiate the racism and some of the cultural incompetence that they faced, particularly in this small town. David talked about some experiences of being stared at. He remembers an incident where he was walking down the street and someone actually said the N-word. There were a couple of racial incidents in high school when his older siblings were there. During the time of his attendance there were also a couple of incidents that he felt were targeted toward people of color in the neighborhood. A couple of times hate language was written on a building, and the community basically came together because they did not feel that it was okay, making their disapproval clear.

David talked about wanting to go to technical school. He was very interested in music—music technology, as a matter of fact. After high school he got a job and then looked into some tech courses. He felt that school did not really prepare him for a productive future. He just felt like he was in a factory, being processed and pushed out. David also critiqued his relationships with his teachers. He felt a distance and a lack of relationship building. He just felt that he was misguided and that his teachers were marginal in steering him toward meeting his highest potential.

That he achieved on his own after he went out into the world as an adult.

Jared

It had been three weeks since I had had an interview with anyone and my deadline to wrap up this project was coming to a rapid close. Twelve stories, varied and similar, took up all of my time with traveling, transcribing, coding, and analysis. Reviewing my field notes, I was able to reconstruct my observations in the field at the sites of many of the interviews. It was all moving along on schedule.

Then Jared called. He had heard about the project and was wondering if it was too late for him to participate and lend his perspective. We agreed to meet at a nearby location. I felt that one more voice could not hurt and in reality could only enhance the initial objective of talking with ten participants. The thirteenth, in my mind, and a lucky number in my life, would be a gem.

I met with Jared and asked him to fill me in on his life here in the Vermont. Jared found it astonishing to be living in a small town within a single-parent household headed by a Black woman finding her way out of rough times and low-income jobs. For Jared, Vermont in its entire splendor had its highs and lows. He talked about his educational career in school and found that by the third grade he was having some prob- lems. Those problems were that he was finding himself in situations where there were some cultural disconnections between him and his teachers, and as a result of those disconnections he found himself in special education classes.

In hindsight, he thinks that his behavior had a lot to do with his frustrations over not being understood, or not feeling included, or feeling invisible. Those seemed to be some of the triggers for him. Those classroom experiences in early elementary education somehow followed him throughout his educational career.

In high school he actually spent most of his senior year away from his graduating classmates in out-of-school suspension. In his last year of school he experienced a lot of isolation, being cut off from his social supports within the school's social circle. It is not that he did not have access to his friends, but that suspension really infringed on his ability to participate in sports and attend school functions. Suspension put limitations on his school-based social life. The life of being one of the big guys on campus when he became a senior was not an option for him. Although he did graduate, he did it through an alternative route. Not having access to his classmates seemed to him, like a punishment. What was really troublesome for him is that there were also students who were White who would act out, yet very rarely did he see them missing in action due to suspension. His being witness to levels of unfairness going on within the school environment was quite troublesome and bothersome for him. At times it angered him. He saw it as racist. After graduating, he landed a job and is working today. Jared expressed that he did not feel as though he was as academically prepared as he should have been to go into a job that is beyond menial wages and manual labor.

Jared attended Vermont public schools. In high school, suspensions and a lack of preparation for a job and career were key drawbacks.

Field Notes: Methods, Observations, and Analysis

Since the state of Vermont was the primary setting for this voice project, included were participants who had gone to school in multiple counties across the state. Within this demographic, the participants were alumni from nine schools, ten different school districts and unions across multiple counties. Their educational experiences were representative of both town and rural schools. All of the participants were post high school.

At the center of this book, are the thirteen young men who identify as African American, Black, or biracial. They were between eighteen and thirty years of age with the median age being 21.9 years. Of the thirteen, twelve graduated with a high school diploma and one, to this date, has not completed his high school education. Students came from predominantly working-class backgrounds; two had a middle-class upbringing, and one had an upper-middle-class background. Nine interviewees had parents who were high school graduates, and three were college graduates. Three of the participants have gone on to community college post high school; one is going to college as a nontraditional student and working; ten are working; and one is (at the time of the authoring of this document) unemployed, yet actively seeking employment in this economic downturn. Five of the participants played a variety of sports and were well known for their athletic prowess. What was the most remarkable about the participants was that they were happy that someone was interested in hearing their insights. All too often when they were in attendance at their respective institutions, their concerns fell on deaf ears. They were happy to share experiences, knowing that their perspectives and feedback might open the door of justice for future students who will be attending schools here in the Green Mountains.

Descriptive analysis requires that the researcher be close to the source when looking for qualitative data. In my search for the subjugated voice of Black males who attended public school in Vermont, I realized I had a big state in which to find participants. Vermont's populations of color live in a variety of locations.

Most people who know me know that my passion revolves around
human rights as they relate to issues of equity and social justice in
education, which are at the heart of my deliberations for all youths. I
asked many people in the greater community, teachers, activists, and
youths I met if they knew any young men who had attended a Vermont
public school, and if they thought these young men might be interested
in sharing their stories with me. After much deliberation in my searching, I was able to make arrangements to meet thirteen young men from
around the state. The method through which I captured their experiences was individual, in-depth, audio taped interviews. A variety of
qualitative methods and analysis techniques were employed to help
ensure trustworthy results. I did anticipate, however, the possible
emergence of a new set of research questions that might have taken the
research to a place needing further study. A comparative analysis of the
participants' experiences may show patterns and themes that are
similar, as well as different in how they experienced their schooling in
terms of discipline practice, suspensions, access to academic enrichment, teachers' attitudes, and levels of expectations for their success.
Prolonged engagement in the field through multiple visits (Gibbs, 2007)
provided the opportunity to keep a constant eye on what may poten-
tially be overlooked or missed in prior visits when only limited contact
with participants occurs.

How did I know, as well as ensure, that the stories I had captured for
this project were valid and authentic to the person disclosing? I validated the data extrapolated from this study by using a variety of analytical techniques, such as triangulation, where participants shared
experiences and perspectives through multiple interviews. After transcription of the interviews, I asked all participants to look over their
transcripts and check for any inaccuracies in our conversations together,
making sure that I represented them and their perspectives accurately
(Glesne, 2006, p. 38). After transcribing the interviews, I destroyed the
taped recordings and stripped all identifiers from the transcribed
documents that were derived from the recordings. All participants were
assigned a numeric code number further reducing any chances of their
identities being disclosed.

Ethics in connection with proper research conduct is not an aspect of
the research process one easily forgets once one has satisfied the

demands of the institutional review boards and other "gatekeepers" of research conduct (Glesne, 2006, p. 129). "The essence of the principle of informed consent is that human subjects of research should be allowed to agree or refuse to participate in the light of comprehensive information concerning the nature and purpose of the research" (Homan, 1991, p. 96). The principles of ethical research are to be traced back to the Nuremberg Code of 1947 (Homan, 1991, p. 96).

In order to avoid harm to any of the young men who shared their perspectives, confidentiality and anonymity were strictly honored. Compared to other states, the size of the African American community in Vermont is small. Thus, I strove in my research deliberations to ensure that none of the participants felt singled out, whatsoever. I also fully understood that if they had had negative experiences in their education, revisiting those experiences might create issues for them. I provided all prospective participants with a lay summary as a way to effectively prepare (Glesne, 2006) them for and inform them of my intentions to use the information gathered in this study. I had them sign off on the lay summary verbally and told them in the summary that they could leave the study at any time—no questions asked.

Lastly, I consistently collected data through the interview process filing them in a thematic codebook until the data were ready for coding upon transcription of the audiotapes. I also maintained electronic files of the transcriptions of the taped interviews. I maintained a complete field journal for field notes and reflexivity in order to create an audit trail in the event that evidence is called for to verify my research data. In order to protect the participants' anonymity, I stored all of my data in a secured, external hard drive specifically designated for this research project. Both the drive and computer are password protected. In protecting their identity on digital media, I also made sure that once the transcriptions were typed and verified, I erased the originals, leaving only transcribed documents. At this point, I coded them to protect each participant's identity. I erased any sign of identifiers (including their voice recordings), which could reveal individuals' identity, and I assigned a numeric code to each participant.

A variety of perspectives collected through taped interviews, provided an ample amount of data to compare and contrast participants' individual experiences while looking for patterns in suspension, low-level tracking, discipline, teacher attitudes, and relationships, as well as paths to graduation and meaningful livelihood. Those patterns, in both similarity and differences, gave me a view into their collective experiences. The method for gathering data utilized multiple collection methods. The main data collection strategy was in-depth interviewing. I was not only seeking answers to my questions, which was vital to the study, but I was also interested in getting to the heart of the participants' individual and collective experiences as males marginalized by race in a state that says everything is all right with them yet has no quantifiable data available to substantiate such claims.

The secondary method of data collection was by examining data sets from the US Census Bureau (United States Census Bureau, 2010), the Vermont Department of Education data on graduation rates (Vermont Department of Education, 2009), as well as reports from the Vermont Advisory Committee to the US Commission on Civil Rights, (1999, 2003). "At the root of in-depth interviewing is an interest in understanding the lived experience of other people and the meaning they make of that experience" (Seidman, 2006, p. 9). The participant interviews all started with the simple question: "Can you describe what school was like for you from elementary through middle school?" This was followed by a second question asking the participants to reconstruct what high school was like for them. Even though African Americans make up just 1.4% of the overall population of Vermont, it was not practical to attempt to observe and interview all males within the state, or even all of Chittenden County. Therefore, the selection strategies I employed were those of "purposeful sampling" and "snowball sampling" (Patton, 2002) of students who have attended Vermont public school (Patton, 2002).

The logic and power of purposeful sampling lie in selecting information-rich cases for study. In-depth and information-rich cases are those from which one can learn a great deal about issues of central importance to the purpose of the research" (Patton, 2002, p. 230). There are sixteen different strategies within purposeful sampling. This allows the researcher to learn a variety of facts about the research topic, and these strategies lead to particular kinds of sites and people (Glesne, 2006). Therefore, the purposeful sampling strategy I intend on employing is referred to as "extreme case sampling," because the research will pay close attention to the school experiences of African American males who have attended, graduated from, or dropped out for a variety of reasons.

"For in-depth understanding, the observer should repeatedly spend extended periods of time with a few respondents and observation sites" (Glesne, 2006, p.36). I met each participant in a private space that was comfortable for him. The creation of a private setting provided the atmosphere in which the study participants gave me an opportunity to gather substantial data to describe and analyze in a cross-case comparative study.

A collective case study for comparative analysis was the best approach for what I wanted to describe and analyze here. I was looking for both commonalities and unique differences in experiences of each of the male participants. Understanding the experiences of African American males who have attended public school in a state that is predominantly White creates a narrative based on their experiences and not only the presuppositions from adults who imagine what their experiences are like. This insight is important, as I stated in the introduction, because much of the research to date is presented to the public from the viewpoint of adults in spheres that are predominantly White as well as historically burdened by their own history of racial inequity.

I would be gratified if the information derived from these stories would serve to inform schools, administrators, and all other stakeholders about exactly what the school experiences of African American males as well as all males of color are like. I want this information to improve the future for students like them. By using case study I hope to make that a reality and a venue for social change. "Case study research is a bounded integrated system with working parts" (Stake, 1995, p. 13). Those "working parts" include the collective voices of marginalized males whose perspectives have yet to be heard in Vermont. I am curious as to how they found their way to success and fulfilling their aspirations in a system that has historically underserved them. It is my obligation as an ethical researcher to honor the participants' voices. Thus, this study is a conduit for their perspectives. I am just providing the medium in which they authentically can be heard.

With Vermont becoming more diverse in its populations of color, qualitative, cross case, comparative analysis provided the window for capturing the multiple perspectives of this group of former public school students. Hearing what members of one of Vermont's most vulnerable populations both feel and have to say about their public schooling experiences lends credence to the public debate about successful education strategies.

Many of my participants had been out of school for an average of three and a half years. What I found curious was that participants were more willing to tell their story after having some distance from their schooling experiences. Students showed more reluctance to revisit their experiences. Only one of the participants was a member of the class of 2010. He was 18 years of age at the time of the interview.

In light of earlier qualitative studies on African American males in New England, this research is unique because it is a baseline, qualitative, study focusing on the lived schooling experiences of this growing demographic population in Vermont. My attempt to add to the body of literature on critical race theory in the context of a just and caring education for all students, especially students of color, is my greatest hope as an outcome for this work. The individual stories of the participants will hopefully impact both meaningful discussion and action on how to contribute to positive public schooling experiences, as well as teacher practice for students of color from now on.

Conclusion

In any situation where one is revealing one's truth the potential to be misinterpreted and misrepresented is always present. And the pushback can be daunting. Sharing requires a level of vulnerability. The young men in this project went to that space of vulnerability to bring to light their lives, in comparison to the lives of other students who look and identify like them in Vermont's public schools. To expose oneself as they did, out in a world that has traditionally excluded them over time, can create all sorts of discomforting issues for the teller, especially when sharing personal histories, when revisiting instances in their lives that may be perceived as emotional or painful. The challenge of going to a place that might have caused the participant harm was always at the forefront of all of my deliberations during this journey.

In terms of sample size, thirteen participants certainly do not represent the experiences of all African American males throughout the state. However, even the voice of such a small segment is representative enough to get some idea as to what school is like for those who identify as persons of color. Because the number of participants in this study reflects only a small percentage of this demographic, it would be misguided to say that what they experienced is common for all students of color.

Nonetheless, the perspectives and voices offer a look into schooling experiences that still holds capital in its universalizable context to the rest of the state as well as region in the context of males of color attending public schools in predominantly White, rural communities.

In the next chapter, "Voices From the Field," the young men will share their public school experiences in a variety of schools around the state.

Notes

1. For more on the national dropout crisis in US public schools, see Children's Defense Fund (2007) and Carger (2009).

2. NECAP (New England Common Assessment Program) scores given in math and reading at grade levels 3, 4, and 5. Scores are given in science at grade level 4. The race data by gender are not visible for the largest diverse district in the state. For more on NECAP, see the web site http://education.vermont.gov/new/html/pgm_assessment /necap.html

CHAPTER FOUR

Voices From the Field

"I felt tolerated but not respected. And the difference is huge. The difference is incredibly huge." (Field note)

In this chapter, I will share with you the various insights and perspectives of the thirteen voices from the field, of the participants taped interviews and conversations around their lived public school experiences across a variety of the states public schools.

It Is Cheaper to Educate a Boy Than to Rehabilitate a Man

Nationwide, approximately seven thousand students drop out every school day, lessening their chances for a prosperous future (Alliance for Excellent Education, 2008). Furthermore, current data on dropout rates pose critical questions that the members of the educational community need to ask with regard to bringing about outcomes that are more just and equitable for all students regardless of their social status. Questions such as, "To what degree can we be more deliberate in making sure data are available in a gender-specific disaggregate, e.g., Black males?" We can get that information on special education and discipline. With a predominance of research focused on dropping out and the rates still on the rise, we should be asking questions as to what might be going on inside the schools that may be contributing factors to why African American and Latino males may be having school experiences that leave many unpleasant memories. What does the research tell us about public schooling from a male perspective?

According to a report by scholar Hal Smith (2009), who brings out salient points in his essay on male achievement in that we must move beyond just seeing success as a factor of individual character or familial circumstance and begin to recognize systemic reasons as well. Indeed, Smith's research is a reminder that responsibility needs to be directed not only at the family but also within the agency most responsible for both systemic and institutional barriers to achievement (Smith, 2009, p. 46). We need to remember that there may be many factors contributing to dropout statistics, and these factors no matter how unintentional they may seem that will have far reaching impact in the life of Black men after high school. Smith suggested that addressing the issues in achievement requires that the educational community take a multidimensional approach to the issues (Smith, 2009, p. 47). I believe we must look at all factors that are barriers both inside and outside of the school, including unexamined bias, colorblindness and cross-cultural competence on the part of adults and others in the environment.

Little had been gained over the past fifty years in terms of under-standing the needs of students of color in order for them to achieve in school. However, many needs still remain unmet in terms of access to safe climate, culturally relevant curriculum, and culturally competent school personnel. These issues are important regardless of where students of color attend school. Small gains in education over the years have been overshadowed by the modern educational achievement crisis. Those gains were influenced by policy and practice that were not inclusive of the needs of students of color and their families. The current movement to create partnerships between families and schools[1] has provided more opportunities for families to be engaged in their stu-dents' schooling, which has made it possible for them to become proac-tive members of the school community. Schools learned that they had to become more inviting to nontraditional families, i.e., more multicultural and inclusive (Nieto, 2000). Given the right interventions, as well as investments garnered from community partnerships, more students can find successful educational outcomes (Nieto, 2007, p. 47).

How do these factors relate to the participants who came from families that were working-class and middle-class backgrounds? Their families' status could not shield them from some of the micro aggres-sions and stereotype threats that unconsciously came their way. Class offers no immunity to intolerance and injustice. Even so, they still persevered. They were resilient. Perhaps it is a coping trait necessary for deflecting the insults perpetrated on their humanity. Sometimes, they were insulted on a daily basis. Not only do males of color suffer from institutional neglect, but they also experience a deep lack of understanding of the unique challenges they face in negotiating school, and of what it means to be a male of color in America.

The results and analysis of the data offer a look into the day-to-day experiences of Black males who are all former Vermont public school students. Like many of their national counterparts, they strove to become educated while overcoming, in some cases, what can be perceived as a lack of care, an unintended consequence of cultural misunderstanding, stereotype threats, and for a few, social isolation. Many talked candidly about their perceptions of the climate at their respective schools and how discipline was handled. All of them had memories to share about life, public school, and being Black in Vermont.

Field Notes and Analysis

The interviews presented the collective experiences of thirteen individuals who attended public schools in a variety of locations across Vermont. Domains that were brought to light in the literature review on Black males and their public schooling experiences were analyzed through the theoretical lens of critical race theory (see Chapter Two). These domains provided a framework for themes that emerged from the data coding: discipline, climate, teacher relationships, and the academic and extra curricular environment.

Finding former students of color who identify as Black male, willing to give interviews, much less willing to share schooling experiences, made me think deeply and long about how I would find, much less approach, young males who would be remotely interested in trusting my mission. Many conversations and much arduous searching ensued, encompassing speaking to many people in the community (both current and former members) about seeking participants willing to answer some important questions about school. After finding the first participant, the journey started to snowball, leading me to find many willing young men ready to share their insights and wisdom about school. The snowball effect eventually led me to a total of thirteen participants. Many of the participants were out of school for an average of three and a half years. The sample, although small, represented a total of ten different school districts and unions across Vermont. What I found very interesting was that the participants were willing to tell their stories after having taken some distance from their school experiences.

Voice out of the Shadows of the Green Mountains

Let me begin by making it clear that respondents are represented by a numerical code in order to protect their privacy. Because I hold the belief that voice is a deeply personal aspect of identity, the participants' responses are exactly as they were recorded in their own words. With the data collected from the field, I initially transcribed each interview by hand. The rationale for this was that line-by-line coding of each sentence in the transcripts provided an opportunity for me to get a closer and deeper sense of the conversations, thus facilitating an opportunity to obtain an understanding of the who, what, when, and why involved in the reconstruction of each participant's experiences across cases.

In order to identify relevant categories that relate to the interview questions, I was dependent on open coding (Gibbs, 2007). Once the interview questions were aligned with categorical codes and the axial coding was refined (Gibbs, 2007), a deeper level of understanding of the connections and comparisons in the experiences of the different subjects became clear. Finally, selective coding helped in the identification of experiential comparisons and contrasts in each participant's experience.

Performing this step in the process, although tedious, kept me close to the data from the onset of being in the field. It also allowed me to create a hierarchy of possible codes aligned with the domains outlined in the critical race theory literature on Black males and their public schooling experiences. I found this process very useful in setting up codes for the thematic codebook as well as providing preliminary codes for analyzing the data through the CAQDAS.[2] Each time I revisited the data, I was able to find new themes—thus meanings—to contextualize as a cross-case comparative analysis. After multiple passes over the thematic codes that emerged, they were then refined using CAQDAS.

The data were then collapsed, creating twenty themes aligned with the domains cited in the literature on critical race theory of education. Within this final set of codes, a unique theme emerged that was generated through a theme builder in CAQDAS. Across all cases, this theme emerged, showing up time and time again when respondents used the term "racism" or "racist" in the taped and later transcribed interviews. I will discuss this theme at the conclusion of this report on the data analysis.

Table 4.1. Frequency Report.

Total	Min	Max	Mean	Std. Dev
Discipline				
Planning Room	1	0	1	0.0770.277
Suspensions	6	0	2	0.4620.776
Academic				
Environment				
Special Education	5	0	1	0.3850.506
AP and Honors	4	0	1	0.3080.48
No AP and Honors	9	0	1	0.6920.48
School Didn't Prepare	11	0	2	0.8460.801
School Prepared	3	0	1	0.2310.439
School				
Relationships				
Teachers	9	0	4	0.6921.182
Teacher and Blacks	11	0	3	0.8460.987
Teacher Impact	15	0	3	1.1541.068
Racist Teachers	3	0	1	0.2310.439
Climate				
Hostile	14	0	3	1.0771.115
Safe	7	0	2	0.5380.66
Bullying and				
Harassment	3	0	1	0.2310.439
Experienced Racism	62	2	8	4.7691.691
Social Isolation	10	0	4	0.7691.301
Stereotype Threats	4	0	1	0.3080.48
Dropped Out	1	0	1	0.0770.277
Post High School				
Going to College	4	0	2	0.3080.63
Working	8	0	1	0.6150.506
Total:	20	190		

The Frequency Report (Table 4.1) above explains the twenty Themed codes attributed to the participants' responses to questions during the interviews and the frequency of the responses across cases.

They were all referenced for the final coding analysis. To summarize this process, the data addressed the two main research questions:

1. How do African American or Black males perceive their own schooling experiences in Vermont public schools?
2. How do they perceive those experiences in terms of climate, teacher relationships, and support within the school?

A central point that I sought to bring to light is that the perspectives of Black males can be insightful and meaningful in determining what Vermont public schools do or do not do to contribute to the achievement and aspiration goals of this and other male populations. Within this baseline study, I anticipated that related hypotheses and new questions might arise as I interviewed the study participants. Such questions assisted in creating a clearer picture, and at the same time supported the primary questions:

1. How do the participants perceive ways they could have been supported to succeed and aspire?
2. How did they perceive their teachers' expectations and attitudes about them?

What do the perspectives say about the public schooling experiences of Vermont's Black males? In the following sections, I will convey their responses through the analysis of their collective experiences, which emerged thematically from the twelve interview questions posed to them.

Discipline

In the data from this analysis, two themes emerged in the domain of discipline: one around the planning room, and the other around suspensions. Of the thirteen participants interviewed, five talked about their experiences with discipline. Their responses naturally and organically arose from the first question posed to them in their interviews. Following are their unedited responses to the interview question, "What was school like for you from elementary through middle school?"

The planning room

One respondent described discipline as a frequent part of his early experiences in public school here. He became familiar with the planning room in his elementary school years, earning tenure in the room for kids who were bad.

> *"I remember they had this room where they would put the kids in if you were bad. They put me in that room, and they would lock the door. Being there a lot, I especially remember that time. I remember, I knew I couldn't swear at school or in that room, but I would swear, and then they would keep me in that room, I was so mad about that."* (Participant 1)

Suspensions and expulsions

Zero tolerance policy has created tremendous controversy over the years due to the racial disparities in both suspension and expulsion rates (Reyes, 2006). Research on zero tolerance policy, school suspensions, and expulsions tell us that African American and Latino males are more likely to be suspended for minor infractions such as violation of dress codes or making a toy gun out of paper (Skiba & Rausch, 2006).

Exclusionary practices are not the best way to deal with discipline. Not only do suspensions and expulsions take away from valuable learning time, but they also create social isolation for the student. For clarity: suspensions are a means of removing students from the school for a short amount of time. Suspensions are the most widely used disciplinary procedure in schools today. Expulsions are used less frequently. Usually, the school board and the superintendent make decisions. Expulsions can be anywhere from a semester during a school year to a full school year or even longer. Boys are more likely to be suspended or expelled than girls (Skiba & Rausch, 2006). Both suspensions and expulsions are the pathway to dropping out (Ekstrom, Goertz, Pollack, & Rock, 1986).

Statistics from the Children's Defense Fund's report, "America's Cradle to Prison Pipeline," showed that in Vermont

- For every 100 White students enrolled in the public schools, there were 4.0 suspensions.
- For every 100 Latino students enrolled in the public schools, there were 4.1 suspensions.

- For every 100 Black students enrolled in the public schools, there were 5.8 suspensions (Children's Defense Fund, 2007).

These are some sobering statistics for a segment that makes up only 1% of Vermont's total population. Without disaggregated data, we are once again unable to decipher how these numbers relate to Black males. Why is there such a disparity?

Three respondents reconstructed their own brushes with the consequences of suspensions in their schooling.

One respondent talked about suspension as an option for redeeming himself and still being able to graduate. The cost: social isolation from his cohort of peers during his senior year.

"I just barely graduated. I had this roundabout way to get out of school my senior year. They had wanted to kick me out for some time. Remember, all the problems I had in school were social and usually with teachers." (Participant 1)

Another describes how his responses to incidents of racial bullying and harassment triggered his suspension. He became the scapegoat for the act of fighting; his claim of racial harassment went unattended.

"I started elementary school . . . there was a lot of, I wouldn't say so much racists or racism but . . . there was a lot of irrelevant name-calling such as the word 'nigger' a lot, so I got suspended a lot for fighting with people calling me 'nigger.'" (Participant 10)

Another talked about his experience during his junior year as nothing short of a forced sabbatical. He was expelled his junior year.

"They chased me through the whole building, just me! I was with two other White kids and they just chased me. Both of them got to stay, I was the only person actually and they told me they wouldn't kick me out, but they said, 'You do have to leave the school.' I came back my 12th grade year and graduated." (Participant 11)

One participant found out the hard way, when his options for future college plans were disregarded due to unthinking, misguided dialogues as well as low expectations from administrators regarding which classes he should take. A noteworthy element missing from the respondent's dialogue with administrators was the presence of a parent.

> *"I got kicked out of what was it? Social studies. And I went to the principal's office and that's when they came up with this whole thing about whether I wanted to go ahead in the class that I was in or if I wanted to go into an easier class. Obviously I'm going to choose the easier class, so after that they put me in a special educa- tion class, that's where the kids that didn't listen went, in there it didn't give me any way to go to college. That topic was- not on the table."* (Participant 12)

Field note

In her essay, "I Don't Understand Why My African American Students Are Not Achieving: An Exploration of the Connection Among Personal Power, Teacher Perceptions, and the Academic Engagement of African American Students," Verna Cornelia Price (2006) asked some thought-provoking and salient questions as she worked with teachers in a large, urban public school district and struggled with student achievement. One question connected to her observations in this school was: "Do we have a system in which students are underachieving or in which teach- ers are underachievers?" (Price, 2006, p. 123). Price's question led to the exploration of the connection of social systems within the classroom, teacher perceptions of students, and the level of positive personal power displayed by the teacher; all these factors are elements that impact the learning and social environment of the classroom and students' learning outcomes. The goal Price sought was to get teachers to think about who they were and the power they held in shaping student perceptions of self and others.

In my personal experience working with in-service teachers, I have always found it curious that when prompted (through an identity activity) to describe their own personal understanding of themselves in relation to their commitment to teaching students in diverse classrooms, the responses reflect either an understanding of or disconnect about diverse students. The rejecting response was more likely to come from those who had no sense of their own racial and cultural identity and whose socialized belief systems about the "other" were being chal- lenged. It was imparted to them as a feature connected to their own personal power as White teachers who impact student outcomes.

One example was a pre-service teacher who had no interest in understanding self through the lens of identity. In addition, there was adamant insistence on the part of this person on not seeing differences between students culturally and racially. This individual thus failed to realize that these attributes are relevant to teaching. What was primarily important to this pre-service teacher was "morality." In other words, the focus was on teaching students moral behavior rather than on teaching them from a culturally relevant pedagogy. In response, I asked this teacher one question: "What gives us the right as teachers to assume that students come into classrooms without any moral foundation?" I felt I needed to challenge this person's assumptions about students before they would step into her classroom. It is this kind of flawed thinking that adds to Price's notion of "teachers as underachievers."

Price is on point when she says that knowing oneself naturally leads to understanding the powerful force called "personal power" (Price, 2006, p. 124). If teachers are unclear about whom they are, as actualized persons, they are likely to project their personal self-doubt onto their students. Teachers who posess a grounded understanding of their own selves and their personal power, can utilize this self-awareness to guide students in using it for their own benefit (Price, 2006). This reflection of power will be evident in the classroom and in the perception of the student as well. The teachers' interactions with their students are directly related to what type of powerful persons the teachers choose to be in the classroom (Price, 2006).

Teachers' personal power affects social systems both inside and outside of the classroom. Climate is one system affected by people in the total environment. Discipline is a response to the workings of those systems in action. Classroom social systems are founded on teachers' understanding of who they genuinely are, what they think about themselves and their students, what level of confidence they bring to teaching, and how they choose to use their personal power with the students.

Price's study found that classrooms and the social systems within them had identifiable characteristics revealing four common types of teacher-student interactions that increase engagement for African American students:

1. Academic.
2. Interpersonal/complementary.
3. Constructive/affirmative discipline.
4. Punitive discipline.

The most common interactions with African American students were academic-interpersonal and/or academic-affirmative discipline (Price, 2006, p. 130). What can we take from this research as it applies to the Vermont participants' responses around discipline as students of color in predominantly White schools?

Climate

School climate has been a daunting issue for many schools across the nation. Today students are suffering and dying due to the subordinated status they hold in a society that still is suspicious of difference. Youths are being attacked not only because of their race but also because of their ethnicity and sexual orientation. All of them are social categories that marginalize students and undermine their individual humanity.

All thirteen respondents had a lot to say about school climate. They explained their own observations and perceptions of injustice and unfairness in school. Of the thirteen respondents interviewed, all experienced differing degrees of injustice during their school careers. Seven participants stated that at one point or another they perceived themselves to be safe at school. A hostile environment can be defined as an environment where students are members of cliques, creating social isolation for some. It can also be described as an environment where teachers are unfair in their practices, creating hostility in the ways they are choosing favorites. Following are the participants' responses when they were asked, "What was the climate like at your school?"

> *"Elementary and middle school? To be honest it was what I made of it and I guess I enjoyed it. I had enough support. I had a big enough support system and then, my mom was active in the schools, in the school system, in the schools ass. So, I never felt alone or threatened because I had somebody who had my back, so, I never felt mistreated or whatever the case. If I couldn't handle it, I had my father and my mother, and they would handle it. They did. So that being said, they would handle it."* (Participant 8)

Not all participants had similar experiences. Many had a mix of both positive and negative experiences.

> *"So my elementary school experiences were very good. Middle school had clique issues; kids started developing opinions and emulating things that their parents did or thought, but middle school was still bearable, I guess you could say it was good."* (Participant 3)

> *"Middle school was a little better, though, and the teachers themselves. . . . I don't know but they didn't seem to care about my ethnicity. It seemed as though they didn't really like their job very much. So, you have the teacher who didn't really want to teach, so I don't think my ethnicity mattered. I worked at the same pace as everybody else, and my grades were good enough. So I got along fine. The kids were okay too. In middle school it was okay. High school was another thing. There I'm really different."* (Participant 6)

One respondent shared that he noticed unfair treatment by teachers starting in middle school.

> *"By middle school and high school though, I noticed people were treated really, very differently. As far as I can comprehend, people weren't all getting treated the same. I mean I remember the Black kids and skate boarders, I remember like the teachers were always watching us, just waiting for someone to slip up."* (Participant 1)

Bullying and harassment are at an all-time high (Vermont Department of Health, 2009). More specifically, 24% of ethnic and racial minorities were likely to be bullied and harassed compared to 16% of White students (Vermont Department of Health, 2009). Three respondents talked about being bullied and/or harassed. I think we need to pay attention to the responses our students are sharing. We must look at and understand race-based bullying and harassment, and find ways of dealing with this additional, racial aspect of this form of unkindness, rather than seeking only to address bullying and harassment for their own sakes. In other words, bullying and harassment triggered by a person's ethnicity need to be examined through the lens and context of stereotype threats and micro/macro aggressions.

One respondent was called the N-word on the school grounds in middle school.

"Here in Vermont as a young person in school . . . school was interesting too because in eighth grade I got called the N-word right outside of the school building." (Participant 9)

Social isolation

Social isolation is one aspect of the school climate as well as discipline practice. Fitting in has a lot of consequences for the social and emotional growth and well being of any student—especially students of color in predominantly White schools. When these students are the only students in their schools, feelings of being different can be very dominant (Middleton, Coleman, & Lewis, 2006).

Teachers need to be very conscious of this scenario by creating environments that are inclusive and do not put students on the spot. Social isolation can be a result of discipline practice, cliques, structural elements, and the general social atmosphere. By structural, I mean academic level tracking, which most often segregates White students from Black students in the same building (Noguera, & Wing, 2006).

"In elementary I was like pretty alone, but I wasn't alone necessarily. I mean from growing up here I had always known I was different." (Participant 9)

One respondent talked about his experiences moving from an urban school to a rural school.

"I didn't like necessarily fit right in with everybody, so to say. I definitely made friends over time, it wasn't like I mean too bad, normal kids schoolyard stuff; kids were picking on me at the time; some kids would like sucker punch me and stuff. I had to make friends when I went to school in a rural area." (Participant 2)

Another participant talked about how, academically, school was really good for him; the social climate in elementary school, however, was hostile and created a lot of issues for him.

"There were probably about five Black males out of about 1000 students in the school." (Participant 6)

"On the education side of things everything was all right. But, in elementary school I experienced the worst racism. So that basically showed you what kind of environment the kids were brought up in at home." (Participant 5)

Respect is the foundation of any healthy relationship. With respect, the capacity for caring is unquestionably evident (Noddings, 1984). One respondent spoke to the concept of "tolerance" in comparison to the notion of respect. Tolerance is an overly used term in the realm of diversity, used as a "feel good" additive to practice (Nieto, 2000).

Schools have to move beyond tolerance in conceptualization and implementation if they are going to impact the diverse students who attend (Nieto, 2000).

"I felt tolerated but not respected. And the difference is huge. The difference is incredibly huge. The overall climate in general; I mean it's a high school, the overall climate is get into the coolest clique you can fit into. The old stereotypes, if you're willing to sell out in high school, then it can be a great place. If you're willing to sell out and if you're a Black male, you want to wear the pants around your ankle, listen to rap music. It could be great for popularity out the wazoo. You know, otherwise you get ignored, and like when you're in somebody's face, people walk past you and they kind of avoid you." (Participant 6)

"I never really hung out much with people in my school because, I knew that they couldn't relate to me, and I couldn't relate to them. If I did, I knew I would have to dummy down and I never did, I didn't have it in me." (Participant 8)

Teacher attitudes add to the climate at school because teachers often set the tone. If they put out the vibe that certain students are troublesome and always going to do something wrong, students will respond to that message. According to research, dynamics that are cultural can create breakdowns in the classroom (Hancock, 2006).

"You could tell that some of them were more like jailers. Which is a problem for me. In some of the schools, a lot of people were more interested in trying to maintain order than having the kids learn anything. Which is a big deal, because you can have all the order you want and you can keep them under lock and key, but if you're more concerned about, you know, maintaining and keeping order and staying in charge, that's doing them a disservice because the teachers are forgetting to actually teach. The main issue here is the interest in maintaining order." (Participant 7)

The adults in students' lives send messages about how to accept difference—from school employees to community members who also have access. One respondent talked about how as a young student a parent tried to clear up another student's questions about racial difference, but in a way that spotlighted his difference. Here is what a few respondents had to say about being different in school.

> *"There was this time I was walking into the library, and this little kid, he was maybe like my age at the time. I was probably eight or nine. This little kid was like pointing at me and said, "What was it?" The mother didn't know what to say. She said, "Well, that's a Black kid," and like, you know what I mean, it was like from that point on. It opened my eyes."* (Participant 9)

> *"'He's Black,' or 'Look at him,' they would say."* (Participant 10)

One respondent was clearly emotional about his experiences in middle school. It is known that the middle-school environment is where bullying and harassment begin to emerge.

> *"My middle school experiences were horrible, horrible; it wasn't even about just Black kids at that point; it was about every kid who wasn't White."* (Participant 11)

Students can experience profiling in the school, especially if teachers are influenced by their assumptions and stereotype Blacks and other marginalized groups. One student talked about being singled out after the interruption of a game that he along with a few White students got caught playing on the school grounds. He paid the price for all three of them.

> *"I would just walk in through the doors and they used to have someone come and check my pockets and made me take off my shoes and check my jackets, only because we got caught playing, a dice game for money, and ever since then they'd been on me; it's just crazy."* (Participant 11)

> *"I got called something derogatory; I can't really remember. I had a couple arguments. Nothing really too serious, although, there was one time I got called something; I can't really remember what they said, but I got called something, and I ended up hitting a kid. I didn't really mean to, but it just happened. You know how it is. It was like segregated in high school."* (Participant 12)

In predominantly White school settings, African American students experience isolation. These are the unintended consequences of a lack of cultural competence on the part of the institutions. Schools with small or emerging populations need to make school not only welcoming but also understanding of students' cultural identities and the histories of marginalized groups.

> *"I mean there were a few incidences that bothered me. I would just go to my mother, and we would just deal with it. I remember we had this play; it was, I think it was, seventh or eighth grade, and it had to do with the Civil War. Me and the only other Black kid in the class were asked to sing Dixie. Nonetheless we didn't sing it, stuff like that, you know. What some people perceive as a problem, some people are asleep, some people just aren't aware. Now granted, my teacher was a fifty-something-year-old White woman and Southern at that. But she didn't know whether or not, you know it was malicious, I don't think so. I think it was pure ignorance."* (Participant 8)

School relationships

Positive relationships in school are important to the success of any student. Teachers are integral to that network of supports along with peers, family, and the community (Hallinan, 2008). Research shows that students are more likely to stay connected to school if they have relationships that are both caring and respectful. Many of the participants had a variety of unpleasant and pleasant experiences with their peers and also with the adults in the building. These ranged from painful experiences that rendered them invisible all the way up to memorable ones that had lasting, positive effects.

The participants may have had some negative experiences but also often had at least one positive interaction with an adult in the school. These positive interactions had not occurred throughout their schooling careers, but when they did, they stood out as having had positive results for them, helping them stay connected to school.

Positive teacher impact

How teachers interact with their students is key to their feeling validated, staying engaged, and achieving goals. The research on student success points to the presence of a significant teacher in their lives (Hallinan, 2008). Individuals who held high expectations for the student, and provided support when needed added to the students' success. All thirteen of the participants described one or two teachers who had impacted them in this sense.

Across all cases, these significant people were central to their schooling experiences. One respondent talked fondly about two teachers who impacted him positively. He shared that, even though he did not do as well in one of a specific teacher's classes, what stood out was the fairness this teacher showed.

> *"Yeah, I had two teachers; specifically I had them my freshman year; these teachers were real cool. One teacher was the only person in the school who I could talk to. I had one class, I probably got a C in his class or something like that; he struck me as someone who was so fair, and I never saw a teacher as being so fair."* (Participant 1)

> *"I mostly got along with everybody and I was kind of comfortable there. I fit in, wasn't really popular at school, but I fit in and it was okay."* (Participant 4)

> *"I was cool with everybody. School was good in elementary and middle. I grew up in the area and my parents did too."* (Participant 8)

Research informs us that Black males in public schools need to have more male role models. This is especially so for those who have no connection to a positive role model in the home or in the community. The research tells us that the teaching force in America is predominantly White, 85% female and middle-class.[3] With such a small population of teachers of color makes it challenging to provide students of color with not only the teachers to whom they can relate, but also teachers who understand them culturally.

The following respondent shared his concerns with having White women as counselors at his school.

> *"We need more people to talk to us students; you know people like me who know what's going on; you know, counselors, anyone I talk to, and this is not bad or anything, but to be honest, all of them are middle-aged White women. I just couldn't vibe with them."* (Participant 1)

Another participant had his perceptions turned around by a White teacher who showed him cultural competence by being caring about his perspective and showing concern when he approached her about a social justice issue that was a major historical event during the modern civil rights movement.

> *"One teacher in my whole life, and I've always said this. In eighth and seventh grade, she, I think, had those qualities. It was during Black History Month, and in the library on display was a bunch of books, different events and important people. I had picked up the Emmett Till story. Kanye West raps about it in one of his songs. And so I went over to her and told her, 'Check this out. These guys are celebrating Till's murder and getting away with it.' This is the first time I heard any teachers swear. She like..., belligerently went off all foulmouthed on the two guys in the photograph. It was like..., wow, I don't know, I didn't feel like all people who were her race felt that towards us but, at the same time to me, especially an older Caucasian lady, it did something to me. It made me feel differently, it opened me up to her more."* (Participant 5)

Another respondent felt that his advisor had a great impact on him as an example of care and respect.

> *"I feel my advisor impacted me the most, in a positive sense. He was a great example. Really I think it was only just him who impacted me. I dealt with him when issues came up."* (Participant 2)

Respect is key in establishing relationships on any level.

> *"Administrators, two of my teachers, out of many core classes, those two were very amicable. When I first started freshman year they were very respectful. I actually developed a relationship with them."* (Participant 3)

Not only does respect fall on the classroom teacher, but the principal or assistant principal are important in maintaining safe levels of climate through advocacy on behalf of students (Reyes, 2006). When there are problems with climate, it traditionally has been the principal or the assistant principal who handles such issues. One respondent shared how leaders in his school helped him negotiate some problematic issues with a classroom teacher.

> *"It really wasn't a teacher. It was the principal and assistant principal. Those were the two people in the school who respected me, honestly. I respected them also. It wasn't just because of their authority; it was because of the way they acted, because they actually were doing something for me."* (Participant 9)

One respondent described what he thought was important for students marginalized by race: someone to whom they can relate.

Black students need to see themselves reflected in the person who is teaching. A shortage of Black teachers of Black students since desegregation has been the biggest hardship for African American students in America's public schools (Delpit, 1995).

> *"A good teacher is a person who understands where you come from and who you are. And what you're trying to achieve, and knows your background, kind of comes from the same back ground as you and if the didn't, they're still trying to help you out; like I had a teacher—he was the only teacher who tried to help me. All I knew is he really wanted to help me go somewhere; he helped me get free college classes and all that. That's the only teacher I would shake hands with today."* (Participant 10)

Teachers and Black students

Participants' perceptions of some of their teachers across cases were pretty consistent in terms of how teachers treat students who are non-White in their schools. Issues emerging in the data analysis ranged from personal interactions, to putting students on the spot if they had academic struggles, to reading out loud, and what it meant to be a Black athlete in a predominantly White campus. One respondent shared his experiences with teachers' micro aggressions, questioning their trustworthiness to do the right thing in school.

> *"In school and in social situations I was always on the margins. I remember the coaches were such older Vermonters. They really didn't want the Black kids at school to play, it seemed. They, well you know, my two friends were all right; they let them play . . . but the other Black kids, they wouldn't even give them a chance. . . . I hated that. There was no fairness, at all."* (Participant 1)

Another respondent talked about the invisibility he felt in the classroom, projected onto him by his teacher when he was the only Black male in his fifth-grade class.

> *"One teacher in the fifth grade probably was not trying to invest as much time in me as the other kids, you know. I brought that issue up with my mom and she*

said, 'All right you're being home-schooled this year.' That's what I did that year."
(Participant 7)

One respondent who identified himself as biracial talked about the challenges he faced once his Black mother showed up at school. His explanation was rather intriguing.

"A math teacher used to dislike me, and the funny thing is, it wasn't until he saw my mom. It's one thing if you can totally pass for being white; it's completely different until mom comes to pick you up." (Participant 7)

Athletes who excel on the sports field are usually bombarded with all kinds of offers from colleges, and the study participants expressed frustration with teachers and their coaches who they perceived to be resistant to them getting these offers.

"I had letters from colleges to go play ball, run track and field; all of that. Nobody ever looked at the letters; nobody ever helped or took one look at the letters. They said, let your mom look at this. My mom doesn't know anything about this, she's from another country; she just graduated high school at something, you know; it took her a while. You know, she didn't know what to do. The White kids, they had them in the office and it was like 'let's do this' and me, they were, I got four letters telling them I want this kid and they say, ask your mom to help you." (Participant 13)

"If you were on the basketball team, you were good for that season while basketball lasted. But when basketball season was over you went back to being no one." (Participant 11)

"I thought they were overly nice to me because I was Black and athletic." (Participant 12)

"But what was funny was that I was the best track runner in the state, all right; so from fall through winter he'd be on me. At one point I wasn't even allowed to walk with my friends after lunch, I had to go from the first floor the other way to go up the stairs. As soon as track season was here I was allowed to run through there, do back flips through the air, jump offs; he didn't care as long as I was running that track and field. But when it wasn't and track season was over I was his worst enemy, at track season the coach, I could do whatever I wanted that was one thing I remember. He was straight up racist." (Participant 10)

Field note

All the study participants talk about interactions with teachers or other leaders in school who had the responsibility to guide them, but instead kept letting them down. The power of teachers' action or inaction and their words have a deep impact and influence on students' identities as well as their learning (Gay, 2010). Teachers need to understand that they are, in a sense, the students' surrogate parents, and they have an obligation to treat all their students fairly and with respect and dignity. Students understand when they are being treated unjustly, and they are aware how racism plays out on both individual and institutional levels. Teachers should see students as their own children and become as vested in their best interest as they would if they were their own.

Academic Environment

In the domain of academic environment, multiple themes emerged out of the data, including special education, AP and honors courses, and preparation for life post high school. The question asked of the interviewees was, "Were you encouraged to take AP or honors classes?"

Of the thirteen participants involved in the study all but one had received a high school diploma. The majority obtained their diploma through the traditional method. By traditional, I mean they participated in the school during their senior year with their cohort and graduated. The themes on special education and access to enrichment such as honors and AP courses was disconcerting, to say the least. Some respondents were frustrated by the missed opportunity to go to college, especially since they were courted by prospective colleges through their athlete status as team players.

Special education

Statistics tell us that Black students, particularly males, are three times as likely as White males to be in a class for the educable mentally retarded, but only half as likely to be placed in a class for the gifted (Ford, 1995). This is abysmal and shameful in a nation that prides itself on being the land of opportunity for all.

Not only are Black students under-enrolled in gifted education programs, Black students are also overrepresented in Special Education, in the lowest ability groups and tracks, and among high school and college dropouts (Ford, 1995, p. 235). One of the thirteen respondents stated:

> *"It's also about what classes they want you to go to. If you come into school, they already had your classes set up for you, my freshman year I remember coming into school thinking I was going to be in all my friends' classes, but it really wasn't like that, it was you're in a special education class. It was basically like that; some kid who was smart, but I couldn't take regular classes, and I don't know why?"* (Participant 11)

AP and Honors

Disparities in gifted and talented placement for Black males, in comparison to White males are high in many of Vermont public schools (Schott Foundation for Public Education, 2010). The following responses were solicited when I asked the participants whether they were encouraged to take honors and AP classes. Of the thirteen interviewees, only four were offered the option by a teacher in the school. Out of the four who were encouraged, only one respondent actually participated in an honors or an AP class.

> *"I was invited into one class. I volunteered for two others, but the only one who encouraged me and said 'you have to go to the honors class because it's this class that you are in right now that doesn't work for you.'*
>
> *That was the only instance. Which worked out pretty well for me."* (Participant 6)

The other respondents, who were all athletes and had been encouraged to take advanced courses, shared that the burden of academic work, a demanding sports schedule, and other responsibilities would have interfered with them having to maintain the grades they needed to graduate. Many students who are from a working-class background have obligations not only to school, but to their family and the community as well.

> *"I was never encouraged to take those classes. I probably would not have taken them anyway. It just never would have happened. But no, I was never encouraged to take AP or honors classes. You know it's pretty hard to get your work done when you have sports; I would come home pretty much exhausted and try to do a little homework, and you know with sports I was done."* (Participant 1)

One respondent, who stated that he, was always resistant to many of the structures and practices in school, talked about the curriculum. His response to the question about AP or honors classes summed up his opinion about the idea, if he had been given the option.

> *"What? No, no I don't think so. Like I said I wasn't following their curriculum. I don't think that was even an idea for any of them, none of them thought I was dumb, but they knew I wasn't going to do the work, so no, I wasn't."* (Participant 8)

A few others talked directly about the curriculum content and how bothersome it was for them.

> *"The use of the N-word in class while discussing the book should have been an unbiased atmosphere, but when you have a bunch of White kids and one Black kid in the classroom it doesn't seem that way."* (Participant 2)

> *"My English class was out of hand. Like it was out of hand. I don't know how anyone made it through that whole year, how anybody passed that class. I passed that class; of course I did my work, but it was like way out of hand all the time. If you are a White teacher teaching to an all-White class, and you have one Black kid in your class, watch out, 'cause he's there. Like if what you are teaching is some racial stuff, like the Holocaust or something, you have to be sensitive to the people in the room; you know what I mean? Know how to present it in a way that doesn't offend. I know history is hard to present without offending someone, like guilt when talking about slavery, the Holocaust, all these events."* (Participant 9)

Many of the other respondents expressed their surprise that there were even such course offerings as honors or AP.

When I asked one respondent if he had been encouraged to take honors or AP classes, he responded in the following manner:

> *"Honors classes? I didn't even know they had those!"* (Participant 4)

Another respondent stated that he had not been encouraged to take honors or AP courses. His perception of teachers' lack of belief in him illustrates that teachers' expectations toward Black boys and adolescents are quite low to nonexistent.

"Nope. Not, many teachers believed in me. Teachers were there to get that pay-check. Their pay was important. They're not really like, interested. I want to help these Black or poor White kids was far from their minds." (Participant 2)

In order for teachers to have the attitude that all students are able to succeed, the teachers need to see not only White students beyond the lens of deficit thinking, but also the students of color. Teachers send both implicit and explicit messages to students that can undermine their sense of identity. Participant responses address those factors.

An overarching theme emerged in the data analysis. All of the thirteen respondents revealed, in one way or another, which they had experience with racism regardless of whether it was in the form of stereotype threats and micro aggressions, bullying and harassment, discipline practice and suspensions, curriculum, teacher attitudes, or behaviors perceived as unjust and unfair. The frequency report shows that sixty-two responses across all cases demonstrate that they experienced some form of perceived racialized slight in their school environment.

In the classroom environment everything is influenced by culture, and our judgment and assessments regarding the classroom interaction are largely influenced by the cultural values we hold (Irving, 2006). Some of these values influence teachers' views on how students and teachers should dress, the appropriate tone of voice students should use, and students' appropriate responses to direction (Irving, 2006). Irving further posited that some factors that contribute to student school experiences that trigger negative outcomes can be identified by teachers themselves, yet they often fail to recognize perhaps the most important factor, the teachers' internal biases and susceptibility to stereotypes in both perception and interaction with students of color (Irving, 2006, p. 195). Often teachers are unaware of how their values, norms, beliefs, and the limited time they spend reflecting on said cultural beliefs and biases create a cultural disconnect between themselves and students who operate from a different cultural paradigm (Irving, 2006, p. 196). Unless teachers (both pre-service and in-service) participate in self-reflective practice that calls them to investigate their internal biases and resistance to working on behalf of all students, students of color will continually be affected with negative outcomes and experiences from their teachers' conflicting cultural paradigms.

This information is a wake-up call to the unfinished business of confronting racism in all of its forms as evidenced in public schools. One interesting claim made in the reports of the Vermont Advisory Committee to the United States Commission on Civil Rights (1999, 2003) was that key members of the educational community, who were integral in the conversations on racial bullying and harassment in schools, did not find it important to be at the table (1999, p. iii; 2003, p. iii). This inability of those in places of power to see and acknowledge that racism exists in Vermont is a testament to the endemic nature of color blindness, denial, and cultural incompetence within our institutions.

Furthermore, I reiterate that this is not a condemnation of teachers, because not all teachers feel this way. It would be closed-minded and naive of me to believe so. I know many genuine, caring and inclusive teachers who are activists for educational and social justice. There are educators across the state doing phenomenal work that is intentional in making the schooling experiences of all students meaningful as well as preparatory. Their commitment is important to helping students become culturally competent citizens in the global environment.

However, there are individuals in places of leadership as well as authority who need to hear, understand, and embrace this imperative as an opportunity for equitable school transformation.

Field note

What has been brought to light through the authentic voices and perspectives of Vermont's former public school students is that even though Black males are graduating from high school here in Vermont, many of them voice concerns about feeling unsupported in actualizing their dreams through schooling. Their stories also expose their individual personal strengths, found in their own agency and deliberations, which allow them to find meaning in their respective educations. According to the participants themselves, not all students were treated equally, equitably, and justly. I hope that this assessment is a wake-up call to those who say they are interested in co-creating excellent and equitable schools that serve the aspirations and dreams of all students.

Field Notes: Reflection

After the interviewing of a small segment of Vermont's emerging African American population, it was clear that men between the ages of eighteen and thirty who had previously attended Vermont public schools had been excited about having their perspectives sought. The findings in the data analysis reveal a plethora of descriptors addressing their issues many that align within the domains outlined in the literature review. The data analysis points to the concerns that still persist in Vermont public schools serving marginalized students. Many of these concerns were highlighted thirteen years ago when the Vermont Advisory Committee to the U.S. Commission on Civil Rights (1999) revealed in their report that racism was apparent in Vermont's public schools, as well as in the state in general. The issues of discipline, climate, and relationships with teachers and other adults in the school are common to many students of color in predominantly White schools. All thirteen participants were given the same set of twelve questions.

The following findings are what came out of the questions in the individual interviews. The first question asked the participants to describe what elementary school and middle school were like, followed by questions about the participants' high school experiences. The subsequent inquiries involved questions about the climate in classrooms, teachers' style of classroom management, and what they considered the qualities of a good teacher. Did they feel prepared for the future, and what would their ideal school look like?

Following are the findings of the data analysis of the participants' responses according to the themes that emerged from the questions.

Discipline

Of the thirteen participants, six talked about their personal experiences with school discipline. The "planning room" and suspension were common themes in these participants' descriptions. Participant 1 talked about his time in the planning room during elementary school, and how angry the experience made him. By the time he reached his senior year, he spent much of his time in school in isolation, from the rest of his cohorts. He was permitted to march during the graduation ceremony, however. This experience reflected a rare break from his isolation at school and from school suspensions. Furthermore, this observation offers a look into the policy and practice of some schools that literally discard students off campus as a form of punitive response to both perceived and real misbehavior.

A more restorative approach may have held more impact. One particular participant could have given me more information, but what I take from the conversation is that from the onset of his elementary education, the norm for him was social isolation. Schools and administrators need to be more mindful of the messages that they give young males of color when their whole understanding of school discipline is punitive and not restorative. Today, it seems, many elementary schools are trying new forms of positive behavior interventions. In addition, the "Responsive Classroom"[4] reflects more of a restorative strategy for dealing with behavior issues. Research tells us that one of the major factors pushing students of color out of school is harsh and unjust discipline practice imposed on them.

Climate

Climate appeared to be one of the biggest domains that emerged from the data. Responses emerged when the participants were asked what the school climate was like. From the responses, seven codes appeared in this particular domain. Whether or not they had a safe or hostile climate in their schools, whether bullying and harassment were present, whether they experienced stereotype threats, racism, or social isolation as an effect of climate—all emerged from that one particular question.

Of the thirteen respondents, half spoke of what they perceived to be hostile environments in school, and half felt safe. There were three responses mentioning bullying and harassment, social isolation, or the perception of experiencing racism. These issues were quite central to this question on climate. Social isolation (Middleton, Coleman, & Lewis, 2006) is another issue that students of color experience in predominantly White schools. Feelings of being different and being the only student of color contribute to those perceptions. All of the participants talked about one form or another of feelings associated with isolation. Exemplary of this situation is coming to a new school and trying to "fit in," which was a term for experiencing social isolation. Some students also mentioned cliques in their respective schools that were exclusive due to many social factors. Hence social isolation, intended or unintended, was not uncommon. Athletes addressed the pressures they experienced, for example, matters of popularity and academic achievements, issues that come along with being an athlete in a sports-centric high school. Stereotype threats also appeared in the responses with athletes discussing the dynamics of being a Black athlete in a predominantly White school or their experiences during the on-season as well as off-season, and the inconsistencies of treatment from teachers during these time periods.

Academic environment

A clearer picture of their academic environment also emerged out of the conversations with the participants. Many of them talked extensively about special education and how they noticed that a predominance of students of color existed in the lower-tracked classes. When it came to AP and honors classes, participants talked about AP and lack of access to them: only one of the thirteen participants in this study took advantage of advanced placement opportunities. Nine respondents out of the thirteen talked about not participating in either AP or honors classes because they didn't know they even existed. A few spoke to the fact that they realized the teachers did not have faith in their ability to benefit from the enrichment provided by AP and honors placement.

The more students of color are given opportunities to excel academically and be challenged, the more they will rise to the occasion. We have to see all students as capable of reaching their fullest human potential. We are all obliged to strive to bring that to reality. Educational theorists and philosopher John Dewey (1902/2009) said in his essay on "The School and Society" what the best and wisest parent wants for his own child, that must the community want for all of its children. Any other ideal for our schools is narrow and limited; if it is acted upon, it destroys our democracy (Dewey, 1902/2009, p. 34).

I believe like Dewey that all children and all students have a right to a rigorous, challenging, curriculum—a curriculum that mirrors who they are, their interests and reflects the multicultural tapestry that makes up American life—resonates with ubiquitous truth. And like Dewey we should want this for all of our children.

School relationships

All participants at one time or another experienced racism in their schooling. Some were very expressive about revealing the subtleties of racism, regardless of their class status (Allen, 2010), discussed as the new racism in the form of stereotype threats and micro aggressions perpetrated by both their teachers and peers.

Some of the participants talked about how some teachers treat students of color unfairly. We saw this dynamic in terms of giving equal opportunity during the sports season or putting a student on the spot in front of his peers if he knew he was challenged by reading in public. To some, there was inequity across the board, whether it was special preference during the sports season or harsher treatment during the off-season. Athletes had examples of both good and bad treatment, depending on their value to the school.

Teachers and other adults

There were incidents in high school that made some of the participants of this study believe that some behaviors toward them were caused by stereotypical beliefs about them. To be leaders in a school, regardless of one's assigned duties; all adults need to be responsive to the needs of all the students. Some student athletes, for instance, were given college opportunities, and coaches did not help them, but still sought them out to make the school team shine. This is nothing less than abusive. If a coach genuinely did not know the drill, then he could have directed the student to the proper channels where such precious opportunities for higher education would not go to waste. These are just a few incidents that speak to unfair situations in our schools. They need to be addressed if racial justice is to occur.

Many civil rights groups have made attempts to mobilize the community in addressing racism here in Vermont. Unfortunately, few identifiable, key players have come to the table. The failure to discuss the issue when it first came to the attention of the public can be characterized as a missed opportunity. Although the participants of this study lived in a variety of places across the state, they shared similarities and contrasts in their experiences. The lack of interest by some school personnel seems to be the result of a combination of color blindness and cultural incompetence.

Unless the community members come together in a united fashion and tackle the issues of institutional racism, the schools will fall short of meeting the needs of all students. Not meeting the needs of all students translates into economic as well as social problems in the greater community. It is evident that the students themselves are not the problem: the data tell us that all but one student made it to graduation, but after high school, they had to pick up the pieces in order to put themselves back on track.

We, who care about education for all, need to put our money were our mouths are, and should not remain silent on an issue about which we can do something. Unless there is a concerted effort on the part of communities, schools, and the leadership within them to talk about White privilege and racism, we will be at a loss. All of us should be uncomfortable with the current arrangement: to refuse to work on solutions is a disservice to all students—not just students of color. The new face of Vermont will not be the traditional one, and students who will become leaders, teachers, and members of the greater community need to be prepared in the correct fashion in order to treat all students fairly and without prejudice using the proper vocabulary.

Becoming an Antiracist Educator

While I believe all students along with their families need to take responsibility for their learning, the reality is that it must be done with the support of those at home and in the school. All of the participants in this study had someone from their home and/or their community to advocate for them at school: folks who were there to reach out to the school leadership on their student's behalf.

We must look beyond the numbers and hear what former students are saying as we prepare for the influx of new faces, languages, and cultures in this once predominantly White landscape. With this growth in cultural, racial, and linguistic diversity, we must be prepared to talk with the people who will make up an even richer environment of cultural pluralism. We need to address the issues we hold precious, and discuss the matters that have been in the way. We must talk about race as if our lives depended on it. There needs to be a priority for professional development for administrators and in-service teachers. If teachers and administrators are to be prepared for the emerging populations that will be the new face of Vermont, they need to abandon these sincere fictions they keep telling themselves and get to the work of being twenty-first century educators (Bell, 1992).

They need to be educators who see, understand, and respect all students as well as their cultural identities. How can Vermont's educators achieve the level of competency necessary to meet students' needs? They must start with themselves, examining flawed perceptions in light of recent research, and choose to improve their teaching service to schools and their communities. The best of intentions are a good start, but today the best intentions are not enough (Ladson-Billings, 1994). We are running out of time. We must be deliberate in all of our intentions as leaders, administrators, teachers and staff.

Administrators

Kailin's (1999) Lakeview research study focused primarily on the in-service teacher as the variable in better understanding race and racism in the school environments where they teach. The research examined the contradictory ways in which White teachers perceive the problem of racism in their liberal community, as well as its effect on their own work with diverse students (Kailin, 1999, p. 726). What I found most curious about this particular study is that the site and sample demographics for the study parallel those of Vermont in many ways. For instance, the census information cited by Kailin stated that 98% of the faculty identify as White and teach to marginalized populations that make up nearly 20% of the student body. Both factors are very congruent with demographics in urban areas of Vermont such as Burlington where White teachers make up 98% of the force.

Furthermore, the study's statistics show a rapid growth over a ten-year span with regard to minority students attending the schools. This pattern closely matches that of Burlington in that some schools show racial and ethnic minority populations of 25% or more ("Burlington School District," 2011). The similarity in statistics, however, provides some evidence of the study's universal context for examining in-service teacher perceptions of racial problems in Vermont schools as well. Vermont school districts serving minority populations have a justifiable reason for tailoring professional development training for a culturally competent, antiracist teaching force. It is a national issue all schools should address. "Research studies conducted over the last thirty years have focused primarily on children's racial perceptions and attitudes as well as the socializing factors that contribute to such development" (Kailin, 1999, p.725) Not much of significance has been present in the literature that focuses on how teachers themselves understand and deal with the complexities and problems associated with institutionalized racism (Kailin, 1999, p. 725). The Lakeview study, however, did just that: investigated a sample of 222 White in-service teachers' perceptions of racism. The site was a "liberal," predominantly White, middle-class school district.

The findings were very revealing. The methodology surveyed a sample of 222 teachers with a total of 189 anonymously responding to open-ended questions about race during mandatory, all-school, in-service days. They were asked to address issues of racism, as they perceived it in their own schools.

Data collected from the 189 of the sample responses were coded and analyzed into major themes and then were collapsed into three major categories:

1. Attribution of racial problems to Blacks.
2. Attribution of racial problems to Whites.
3. Attribution of racial problems to institutional/cultural factors.

The analysis of the data revealed "when referring to examples or incidents of racism, nearly all the respondents except two perceived racism to be essentially a Black/White phenomenon" (Kailin, 1999, p. 730). As a matter of fact, a large percentage of the respondents had a real disconnect in understanding an issue that affects people of color. More, specifically, 45.5% assigned causality of race problems to Blacks, 41.6% assigned causality to Whites, and 12.8% attributed causality to institutional and cultural factors (p. 731).

What can Vermont's educational community learn from Kailin's Lakewood study? Leadership needs to lead the engaged journey into understanding race and its historical underpinnings in American education. In order to arrive at that understanding we must talk courageously about race, racism, colorblindness and White privilege. Until race is made visible through investigating our socialized beliefs, color blindness will prohibit true school transformation efforts that are both socially equitable and inclusive.

Teachers and Staff

Climate, the culturally responsive classroom, high academic expectations, and the sports arena play a key role in Black students' schooling experiences and outcomes and are instrumental to success and achievement. As outlined in the body of literature on Black boys and public schools, low expectations along with a cultural mismatch may be contributing factors that lead to Black males' lack of staying connected to school. African American males can have more meaningful and more rewarding schooling experiences if school climate is inclusive and opportunities are equitable. Educators must be willing to gain a deeper understanding of their students as individuals with distinct cultural attributes and consider them as equals to any other student in their charge. Furthermore, respect is important in any relationship. A lack of respect and understanding from teachers and administrators toward students of color can be translated into a lack of caring that is based in the history of dysfunctional relationships across both race and gender.

We can learn what made schools work for students of color, especially since schools today are more segregated than prior to 1954 when schools were forced to integrate. Unfortunately, desegregation basically disenfranchised Blacks from having power and voice in their children's education. Furthermore, historically all-Black schools created a context for caring for all students equally. School was relevant to all Blacks then because there was cultural synchronization (Dempsey, & Noblit, 1996). Teachers and students had a lot in common culturally and racially. Care and justice became inseparable (Walker & Snarey, 2004) when the whole community had a say in the education of the children. This type of situation however, does not exist today. Schools and teachers are still predominantly White. Therefore, parents no longer have much power or voice in their children's schooling and classrooms. Hence, the relational element is missing or lacking.

In order for students to receive a rich and meaningful learning experience, what is needed is a unified system that features the successes of historically all Black schools that made them exemplary environments for all students to excel and achieve academically (Murrell, 2002). Teachers of African American students must be able to understand contemporary educational theory and apply it to their practice while integrating the historical, cultural, political, and developmental considerations of the African American experience into a unified system of practice for educational achievement (Murrell, 2002).

Conclusion

Based on the analysis of the stories of the thirteen participants, Vermont public schools need to become more socially and culturally aware of the populations who will be sharing classrooms with White students. I understand that in some places in Vermont White males suffer from marginality similarly to males of color. Their situations, however, are mostly class-based. Boys in Vermont who are White are more likely to drop out of school if they are in poverty. However, their issues are glaringly present within the states educational data (Vermont Department of Education, 2010).

Seeking to find comparisons and contrasts in the public schooling experiences of Black males has shown that they share more in common with regard to suspensions, climate, and teacher impact than we would like to believe. This inquiry process presented its challenges, but I found it rewarding to connect with males in greater Vermont, who were brave and trusting enough to be candid when sharing their personal experiences with me.

Since some African American males are experiencing the effects of systemic and institutional racism in their schooling, I recommend an ongoing, qualitative, longitudinal study that encompasses the experiences of all students of color in Vermont and their public schooling, in order to further understand how deep institutional racism is in our schools. I am curious as to what the experiences are like for African students in a system that not only marginalizes students by skin color but also by ethnicity and linguistics. In today's social climate, does the double bind of not only skin color but immigrant status affects the experiences of these newly emerging populations?

This exploration into the relegated voices of Vermont's African American males rendered valuable insight into their lived, individual experiences in public school, and also gave me—the researcher—a deeper understanding of both the positive and negative factors that add to their experiences in predominantly White schools. I learned that the support systems from home certainly influence student outcomes. However, success was also affected by climate, which includes administrators, teachers and staff, who see all students' in their full humanity and cultural or racial identity, and hold high expectations as well.

Most importantly, these are the stories of men, mature and strong in their sense of themselves, who are endowed with deep resilience and resistance to the stereotype threats and micro aggressions that engaged them in ways that are unimaginable. However, these young men, many native to Vermont, found redemption by creating meaningful lives for themselves in a place that oftentimes saw them as both strangers and outsiders. Their stories provide us, as a community, with information as to what business needs to be addressed in our public schools. Hopefully, the perspectives of the thirteen participants of this study will help prevent other students who attend public schools in Vermont from experiencing the isolation that marginalization often produces.

In the fifth and final chapter I will discuss my thoughts and insights into making public schools work for all students regardless of their social identity. This vision is geared toward creating meaningful, holistic experiences for African American males as well as other nontraditional students as we prepare for their growing presence in our schools and communities.

Notes

1. For more on partnerships between families and schools, see Epstein et al. (2009).
2. CAQDAS (Computer Assisted Qualitative Data Analysis Software). CAQDAS software is used in many fields of study, such as psychology and other social sciences, to assist in qualitative research. It aids in tasks such as coding, transcription analysis, and content analysis. For more on CAQDAS see, for example, the University of Surrey's "CAQDAS Networking Project" at http://www.surrey.ac.uk/sociology/research/researchcentres/caqdas/.

3. For more on the history of relationships between Black males and White teachers, see Hancock (2006). See also current data through National Education Association (NEA) (2010).

4. For more on the responsive classroom, see Charney (1997); Charney, Clayton, & Wood (1997); and Brady, Forton, & Porter (2010).

• CHAPTER FIVE •

From Color Blindness to Color Talk

At the turn of the last century W. E. B. Du Bois (1903/1993) presciently proclaimed, "The problem of the 20th century is the problem of the color line" (p. 15). Perhaps Du Bois's glimpse into the future from where he stood was a cautionary tale assigned to the unfinished business of all things race in American society. Especially within the halls and classrooms of the great leveler: the school building. I often wonder if people of color were ever really considered in that discussion as well? Because the profound words that ushered in the last century seem to have a lingering effect into the new one.

In this last and final chapter I will discuss my perceptions on the state of race and education in our public schools and the imperative in moving the equity conversation along. We have arrived at the moment in which transforming our schools into becoming more inclusive and relevant for the communities in which they serve should have been a priority with the recommendations set forth fifteen years ago by the Vermont Advisory Commission and the Office of Civil Rights. By listening to the messages our youth have to share then and only then can we help the process move from marginality to one of community ownership and inclusion.

The Twenty-First Century and the Color Line

Here we are at the dawning of the new millennium, and from where I stand the color line is still clearly present in the context of housing, health, economics, justice, and education. Hence, equal access to the promises and rewards of public education are pretty much still fiction for the majority of students of color, especially Black and Latino males. Is the national crisis, a reality for males of color here in the Green Mountain State?

Students of color may be graduating as the data suggests, but many are not going off to two-year, much less four-year colleges.[1] If they are going off to college many are not adequately prepared for the rigors of higher education, thus find it hard in attaining a degree. Furthermore, some are also unprepared for jobs or careers that do not require college degrees. We have racial disparities in the Vermont justice system that lead me to question whether the "cradle to prison pipeline" (Children's Defense Fund, 2007) has arrived?

Apart from a single report issued by an educational non-profit outside of the state (Schott Foundation for Public Education, 2010), we have no stand-alone data on Black males, other than data that focus on perceived deficits such as special education, suspensions and discipline, and lack of access to honors and AP classes. Why is it the case that the state finds it important to compile punitive behavioral and lack of access data, yet finds no apparent need to maintain achievement and attainment outcome numbers disaggregated by race and gender? Are we unconsciously participating in upholding bias perceptions of black criminality and lack of intelligence by focusing on data that can be perceived as such? As for the behavioral data, the Office of Civil Rights (OCR) has kept records since 1997. Can we step back and see the connection between perceived criminality and capturing data focusing on behavior and character? Where are the schools priorities?

When it comes to academic testing data (such as the NECAP standardized testing in both math and reading proficiency that records achievement benchmarks throughout the grades in students' education careers) the race data for both girls and boys are combined. Graduation data give us some information, but not all of the data are reliable indicators as to whether or not a student will end up in the academy, job market, or the justice system.[2] What are we as concerned citizens to take away from this information? Quantitative data has its own story to tell, which can be very useful, but in reality the numbers in Vermont have been inconsistent, inaccurate, and confusing, to say the least.

Are we transparent about the facts on Black and Brown male achievement here in Vermont? Let me be clear that by achievement, I mean not only graduation, but also preparation for a job or career as well. I have often wondered just how well Vermont's young men are doing once they get the diploma. Have they garnered the social and cultural capital to cash in on the rewards that an equitable education has to offer them? The kind of education that prepares their White, middle-class counterparts for gaining meaningful employment, and which constitutes, for some, a foundation for building wealth. Has the playing field become level in Vermont? Have we become so progressive that our schools no longer sort and rank students? Have social reproduction and racism in the schools ended in the Green Mountain State? All of the indicators to date say no, we are not there yet.

Moreover, if we look at the Vermont Advisory Committee to the Human Rights Commission report of 1999 and 2003 on racial bullying and harassment for instance, recommendations were directed to the largest and most diverse district in the state: Burlington School District. Some issues seem to have been disregarded over time. The recommendation to regard the conversation on race and racial issues within the school and greater community is clearly articulated throughout the documents recommendation section. I see this as a means that is key to building bridges across racial difference as well as an opportunity to see diversity up close. Why such resistance to the talk? The "green book" came from the will and concern of the people, with the backing of the Human Rights Commission. Therefore the voice and will of the people has spoken by making it clear that racism is a problem in our schools.

Over time and with some pressure from parent groups such as Diversity Now, community-based equity advocacy groups like VTMADE, VARAT and other stakeholders, the Vermont public now has access to data, released as recently as the fall of 2011, from one of the most diverse school districts in the state. Paying heed to the call by a large stakeholder coalition, the Burlington Board of School Commissioners called for the creation of a Task Force on Diversity and Equity ("Task Force Report," 2011) charged with the specific mission of improving student achievement and creating a more culturally competent and inclusive school community for all students.

Through the collaborative efforts of a broad base of community members, teachers, and stakeholders across the district, the Task Force produced a multi-year strategic plan to further move the district forward in its efforts to make the schools socially equitable. A multi-year strategic plan entitled, "Task Force Report on the Recommended Strategic Plan for Diversity, Equity, and Inclusion for the Burlington School District" (2011) was the final culmination and manifesto of those thoughtful efforts.

Data from the report, however, pointed to some academic and social inequities for students of color throughout this particular district. Inequities that create the disparities that will eventually have a profound effect on students' aspirations, achievement, and attainment.

The data however was not well received by some across the district. Therefore by winter 2012 the school district and community were divided on the issue of race and perception. Some took the data as being wrong because it pointed to racial disparities. Disparities that are inline with those on the national level, that leaves males and other students of color behind. The months to ensue would be tinged with denial, cultural misunderstandings, and fear. My hope is that the reports information is a call to consciousness of the homework unattended when populations of color started to become more and more visible in the community years ago.

What information does the report reveal that has the community torn apart?

In this report the following data emerged:

1. The percentage of White students (7%) taking the SATs or the ACT test was more than double the percentage of students of color (2.9%).
2. In the high school dropout rate a gap of nearly five percentage points existed between students who identified as African American (19%) and those who identified as White (14%).
3. There was close to a twenty-percentage-point dropout rate gap between students who were eligible for free and reduced lunches as compared with those who were not.
4. Black students were disproportionately achieving math proficiency (they were 4% percent of those who were taking and passing Algebra 1) but represented 13% of the student body.
5. English language learner (ELL) students, who made up 17% of district students, were significantly more likely to be found responsible for cheating violations than non-ELL students.
6. Although students of color made up 27% of the student body they were over-represented (34%) in the numbers of those being punished through in-school suspensions.

7. Students of color were extremely over-represented (60%) among those being punished through out-of-school suspensions.
8. Black students made up 13% of the student body, yet accounted for 27% of out-of-school suspensions throughout the district.

What does this data tell us about this school district, and about Vermont public schools and their newly visible populations in general? The data clearly informs us that race is still a factor in the educational outcomes of non-White youth. This data, also tells us that there are some race-based inequities in both discipline practice and suspensions. Have color-blind attitudes and practices along with resistance to talking and acknowledging race as a factor in these social outcomes? I don't really know. I could conjecture and say apparently so.

What the data do not tell us however, are the stand-alone disaggregates for Black males, leaving us, the observers, to infer or guess what may be going on for males of color. Still, I ask how are males of color doing? I also wonder, by the sheer disparity in the suspensions and special education usage, if the indicators point to some factors earlier discussed in chapter two. The Schott Foundation's report, which I discussed in Chapter One, also pointed to similar disparities while still applauding the inverted graduation gap. That is where I see red flags in the data with some concern.

This is not rocket science. In reality, it is plain common sense. To be honest, the evidence had been put before us fifteen years ago. Those who had the power to lead transformative systemic change did not find the issues important enough to even show up at the table. They did not heed the warning. I believe this emerging data will help to expose the negative outcomes that so many have for so long refused to acknowledge. In my mind, indifference and colorblindness are synonymous with apathy. Apathy feeds the elephant has been sitting before us and everyone has been tiptoeing around in avoidance.

Was the 1999 Advisory Committee to the Vermont Commissions on Civil Rights Report on racial harassment in Vermont public schools an unheeded warning, fallen on deaf ears? I believe it was a missed opportunity in preparedness. I don't want to place blame, but the earlier Vermont reports foretold some of the issues revealed in the BSD Task Force Report of 2011. The statewide report from 1997 articulated recommendations directed at the BSD (p. 84). Could the BSD disparities possibly be a result unintentionally overlooking some of the issues, addressed over a decade ago? Could overlooking the relationship between race-based equity in the deliberations be a contributing factor as well? Many of the recommendations outlined to the BSD clearly state that acknowledging race as a factor, which should be part of the deliberations of the district around issues of diversity (p. 84).

It is apparent to me that our struggles to remove race from our collective dialog is a direct result of many in positions of power to unconsciously turn the tides of justice around, by not being aware of race as a factor at all. We do not have the luxury or the time to let that happen in our schools. Remember, back in 1997, families of minority students had concerns relating to many of the recommendations put forth: the use of curriculum materials promoting racial stereotypes; the presumption that minority students are involved in criminal activity; and unsatisfactory, school-based response to racial harassment incidents; and fifth, an overall climate of racism that exists throughout the state (Vermont Advisory Committee to the United States Commission on Civil Rights, 1999, p. 6).

As we consider the evidence put before us in this text by both the federal and state agencies, we are obliged to face up to the fact that racism is an issue in our schools and we must find ways to countervail, minimize and erase it. On both the district and the state levels, Burlington schools need to act on the Task Force recommendations and see them with an urgency that was absent in the past. We need to act and move forward because the future is staring us in the face, now.

Furthermore, in our deliberations for equity, we must not overlook the need for a deeper inquiry into the understanding of the issues that get in the way of the ability of students of color to achieve. If, in comparison to their White peers they are being disproportionately punished for the same infractions, then something is gravely out of balance within the institution. In school transformation efforts we must rethink the outdated traditional methods and practices of educating all of our students (including many who are new to the country), that may not really be suited to their cultural, racial, linguistic, and ethnic trajectories. The one-size-fits-all remedy, enforced by schools does not fit at all. As a matter of fact it is very uncomfortable fit.

When we look at poverty along with race we must consider the perceptions and messages that the curriculum sends to students who exist in spaces of marginality. Students lose valuable class time when they are suspended or expelled. The likely results are that they end up falling behind and dropping out. The same circumstances that are influenced by class, as far as schooling outcomes, are more prevalent for students of color than for their White peers.

Nevertheless, as educators, we are obliged to know and understand the things that spark passion and engage our students. The only way we will discover these things is by building relationships with them. But relationships cannot happen in a vacuum. Therefore teachers must also get to know who they are themselves as raced people. They must explore and engage in their own cultural and racial identity as White and see that their White privilege is a benefit of a society founded on White domination. They must also understand the level of dysfunction in the history of race relations in the dynamic that exists between Black males and White women. Without investigating these factors the road to equity will be littered with fruitless outcomes.

What is the road map to equity for all students, but for males of color in particular? I believe it takes leadership, creating opportunity where none existed before, and praxis. Praxis in terms of applying the theories' grounded in multiculturalism, along with the implementation and application of antiracist, culturally responsive pedagogic practice. But first and foremost the color blinders (the blinders that inhibit some from being able to see race as a factor) must come off and the classist mythology of poverty must be challenged in order to talk about, understand, and actively counter the impact of racism on our children's sense of competency and identity.

To Actualize Justice and Equity for All Students, Please Remove the Color Blinders

Even though some of us would like to believe we have overcome our racial past by embracing color blindness as a marker of our social progress, the information placed before us in this book suggests otherwise. Furthermore, I agree, on one hand, yes, we have come a long way as a nation, including seeing the first African American make it to the highest political office as Commander-in-Chief. Nevertheless, I am of the mind-set that we still have a long, long way to go in bringing equity and justice to communities that are marginalized by racial as well as socioeconomic affiliation. So, how do we actualize equity in a time when color blindness is still as pervasive as it has ever been, prohibiting many from seeing inequity tied to their students' racial identities? I believe we must start with an understanding of the one-hundred-and-fifteen-year history of the color-blind ideology and its confusing interpretations into the twenty-first century.

According to the work of Atwater, color-blind ideology traces its genesis back to the landmark 1896 Supreme Court case of, *Plessy v. Ferguson*, in response to the endemic nature of racial bigotry and hate in the American landscape. Justice John Marshall Harlan argued in dissent: "Our Constitution is colorblind and neither knows nor tolerates classes among citizens" (Atwater, 2008, p. 246).

Over time color blindness became the badge of honor for many in the field of law as the issues of racial inequality came to light. The rationale was that justice should be blind to racial differences, especially skin color. In a perfect world, that idealistic view may apply, but because racism is as much a salient part of our contemporary society as it was in our early history as a nation, it is difficult to be so simplistic in its definition. It is true that we have made many gains since the end of the nineteenth century, but we still have a long way to go in achieving equity in terms of housing, health, and education. Furthermore, so many Americans have embraced this notion of color blindness over time that most have come to believe it, and have bought into a distorted view and interpretation of the meaning. Most Americans, especially White Americans today, have been socialized to believe that "race should not and does not matter." This fits neatly with deeply ingrained American social values and the belief in individualism, which encourages a strong disregard for group membership (p. 247). Individualism and lack of identifying as a group is the foundation of White identity. Subscribing to the notion that race should not matter strongly imply that in the goal of achieving color blindness justice should be blind to skin color and racial differences. In education, however, this means not showing favoritism or discrimination to certain students based on skin color. That philosophical position requires that teachers turn a blind eye to racial differences despite the fact that skin color does impact how individuals are treated in society (p. 247). The racial disparities along many social indicators imply that, even today, racial discrimination is still a critical factor.

Moreover, Williams (1998) cited in Atwater states, "The very notion of blindness about color constitutes an ideological confusion at best, and denial at its very worst. Much is overlooked in the move to undo that which clearly and unfortunately matters just by labeling it that which 'makes no difference'" (p. 247). Many people feel we have truly arrived at this ideal of "race doesn't matter" in our society. Colorblindness is an ideology that has been made normative due to the signing of civil rights acts and other legislation. With the signing of civil rights laws, this idealistic notion that we have arrived at a colorblind society has been embraced, implying that we are all done with the basis of race and that we have closed the books on racial discrimination in this country. The espousal of this odd notion, when we live in a country that still discriminates, creates a flawed view of the world. Social research addresses the detrimental effects to our nation's racial harmony with this embracing of an unrealistic view of race in America.

The scope and breadth of the inquiry also educate us to the fact that teachers often walk into the school space with unexamined, internalized cultural biases already in place that can actually create racial inequities in their pedagogic practice, student expectations, how they mete out discipline, and whether or not they see students as capable of participating in enrichment classes (p. 248). The Atwater study investigated color blindness in schools by asking elementary school teachers to rate eighty-six White and sixty-three Hispanic fifth-grade students on elements of learning, motivation, creativity, and leadership (p. 248). The research findings showed that ratings varied considerably based on the student's ethnic status and their level of acculturation. Results showed that Anglo-American White students were rated higher in positive attributes than their Hispanic peers, and that highly acculturated Hispanic students received higher ratings than their less acculturated Hispanic peers (p. 248). Atwater's study concluded that, "colorblind studies have helped delineate the issues of unconscious biases, the invisibility of whiteness and the privilege that goes along with it as well as the way that color-blindness serves the needs of the teacher to the detriment of both themselves and their students" (p. 252). Hence, internalized biases and socialized assumptions do drive equity at the hands of teachers. In order to arrive at a place of educational equity, I suggest that we pause for a moment of deep reflection. In that reflection we must be painfully realistic with not only ourselves but with each other in understanding that unless teachers (including teachers of color who also acquiesce to hegemonic norms) accomplish the personal work required of them—to be effective educators of the students of this new millennium—the disparities and gaps will continue. Teachers must be willing to gain the skills necessary for deconstructing racialized, classist, and linguistic assumptions about the students they teach, or nothing will be accomplished in the struggle to change student outcomes.

We must look beyond holding just one party accountable for the issues that add to the phenomenon of males of color, new Americans, and English language learners having less then stellar schooling experiences. Most importantly we must remove the color blinders of denial and start talking about race as if our children's very lives depended on it, because in the final analysis, race still gravely matters. Here in the green mountain state we have very little discourse around race and education equity that have led to successful solutions. In our deliberations in overcoming racial bullying and harassment have we overlooked the impact of microaggressions in investigating race based bullying and harassment? Have we learned to truly discern between the two?

Engaging in Color Talk

Both former President Bill Clinton (1995) and President Obama (2008) addressed the need for all of us to talk about our nation's racial history and the lasting legacy of racism. I believe that in many places people are starting to move in the right direction on coming to the table for that conversation, but we still have obstacles to overcome. The task is challenging because the conversation cannot meaningfully happen without the conversant being conscious that, first, racism still exists, and, second, that it continues to be a historically real aspect of the human condition in the schooling experiences for students of color. Lastly, teachers must not take racial inequity as a personal affront to their integrity, but must understand that racism still exists in schools, no matter how unintended.

How do we work with teachers in understanding this reality in their community of colleagues and learners? In what ways can teachers be supported in becoming more aware of race and racism in the school environment? How do we get them to take off the blinders and overcome color blindness?

I think when it comes to color blindness educators must investigate the two conflicted and confused interpretations of color blindness, an ideology that appears to have been socialized into the American psyche, further confusing and confounding the majority of people, and stymieing efforts to undo racism, classism, nativism, and other forms of oppression. But first and foremost we must resolve to take the risk of leading the conversation, no matter how discomforting it may be, in our classrooms as well as our spheres of influence, and we must speak frankly with open hearts and ears.

In order to move forward we must first see all students in all of their social identities, including their race. If you are in the classroom and your teaching method and practice as well as attitude say that you do not see, much less acknowledge, your students' identities, you will do a great disservice to them as a result. In order to unpack the burden of race and racism one is required to take the risk of engaging this issue. Twenty-first-century educators must become more informed about the role that racism still plays in our nation's social institutions. They must also understand the key roles that structural bias and human agency play in perpetuating racial and class inequity, especially in school. Both pre-service and in-service teachers must become proactive in creating more harmony and equity in their schools and classrooms by first seeing the racial identity of students who are in the school and then becoming conscious of racism, not only on the personal level but also on the institutional level.

I realize that mandating that White people do their own personal inventory and self-assessment on their level of race awareness and color blindness can be a bit problematic, especially for educators who have had little to no contact in their socialization with people from diverse backgrounds. I have found that even in my own personal life, where interracial or intercultural relating is a constant given, it is still hard for some White people to talk about race out of fear of discomfort or being seen or labeled as racist. We all must learn to go beyond our comfort zones in order to be present for our students. I have come to the conclusion that many are good at "unintentionally" verbalizing the micro aggressions and stereotype threats, but are lacking in the ability to participate in a dialogue about their own cultural inadequacies. There is an extreme amount of power in the dynamic, especially if it is one-sided and works in favor of hegemony.

I assure you that this is not a blame game. Though, I do admit, however, it is a reality check, a second wake-up call. In my work as an antiracist educator and activist bringing the race conversation to classrooms, I have found that occasionally, a color-blind mind-set greeted me before the readers were even engaged with the reading to the class. On one occasion, a teacher who was well prepared in advance about the antiracism literacy project I coordinate, told the guest reader, "We don't talk about skin color in this classroom." This is a perfect example of the unconscious resistance that normatively persists in many Vermont schools.

I fully understand that conversations about race and racism can be very difficult and complex. Often, talk about race is avoided in the public sphere altogether. Comments such as, "Children do not see race, so why bring it up?" and "I don't see race, I see people" are commonly heard. Color blindness is seen as "camouflaged racism" in a sociopolitical context, said activist and educator, Angela Davis (1997). "Social 'color-blindness' is parasitic on racism and it is only in a racist society that pretending not to see race could be constructed as a virtuous act" (Walker, & Snarey, 2004, p. 24). The impact of color blindness on privileged members of society has been enormously detrimental not just to the development of an authentic self but also in the nation's ability to deal with the legacy of racism. In order to practice true democracy, we must critically talk about the history of racism, legacy of institutional racism and challenge the hegemonic norms of "Whiteness." We must find the courage and backbone to hold these conversations in as many social venues as possible. The biggest barrier to talking about race is colorblindness and fear. You most see first see race in order to talk about it.

Holding on steadfastly to the mindsets of color blindness and denial closes the door to fully actualizing a just society for all children and future generations. The point that I am making is that all children see race (even isolated White children)[3] (Derman-Sparks & Ramsey, 2006), and they are affected by the conflicting messages they receive from both the adults who care for them and from the world at large. These types of messages hinder both social and emotional development. Both Black and White children internalize the racist and supremacist imagery prevalent in society, giving them a false sense of inferiority and superiority from which they judge themselves and others. Unchecked, internalized superiority presents itself in adults as aversive racism.

"In a racist society, Black children cannot be protected indefinitely from the knowledge of racism. Yet White children, because they are not on the receiving end of racism, may remain more or less blind to it" (Derman-Sparks & Ramsey, 2006, p. 26). Color talk recognizes that a person's color is not only a significant dimension of her or his experience, but also of her or his identity (Walker & Snarey, 2004).

In order to overcome the silence that color blindness puts upon people, they must engage at each and every teachable moment in the complexities of color talk. Inviting all children and adults into the province of color talk will benefit them in developing healthy attitudes and behaviors towards difference and themselves. Singleton and Linton (2006) could not have put it more succinctly: To participate in effective interracial dialogue about race, the first step is to commit to the Four Agreements of Courageous Conversation (p. 58).

By committing to these, participants agree to

- Stay engaged
- Experience discomfort
- Speak your truth
- Expect and accept non-closure.

That is one way I believe we can bring to an end the injustices that traditionally marginalized students face in their everyday school experiences. It is vital to engage everyone by inviting them into the province of color talk in order to reverse the negative repercussions that stem from identity invisibility and invalidation in the school environment. If young students across a variety of school districts across Vermont are talking about race and racism, it is now time for the adults to catch up, especially leadership and the policy makers. Colorblindness is not a virtue; anti-racism, however, certainly is.

Antiracism and Culturally Responsive Pedagogy

Teaching across cultures, abilities, linguistics, ethnicity, and race (culturally responsive teaching) (Chartock, 2010) presents a host of new and unique challenges in schools today. Adopting an antiracist identity, awareness, and behavior are key factors to multicultural teaching from the culturally responsive pedagogy (CRP) approach. The importance of learning about these issues and the implications for teachers must be underscored. Aside from twenty-first-century educators having the responsibility to find out about themselves by investigating identities as White, they are also charged with gathering pertinent information about the cultural identities of the students and families they encounter in the classroom and school setting. Adding a culturally responsive pedagogic approach to the multicultural teaching of diverse students brings meaning making to the classroom of learners. Culturally relevant curricula are just as important as the academic and social curricula provided by schools, and are equally vital aspects of every student's academic and social success (Chartock, 2010, p. x).

What does a culturally responsive environment look like? According to the National Center for Culturally Responsive Educational Systems (NCCRESt) the following list represents some things that teachers can do to make their classrooms and schools culturally responsive to the needs of the diverse learner:

1. Validate students' cultural identity in classroom practices and instructional materials by using textbooks, designing bulletin boards, and implementing classroom activities that are culturally supportive. This may mean using supplementary resources that don't perpetuate stereotypes or inadequately represent certain groups.
2. Acknowledge students' differences as well as their commonalities and respond to their individual strengths and weaknesses.
3. Educate students about the diversity of the world around them so all students learn to relate positively to each other regardless of cultural and linguistic differences.
4. Promote equity and mutual respect among students in ways that a) ensure fair treatment across all groups and b) carefully moni-

tor behaviors that are traditionally rewarded to ensure they're not culture bound.

5. Access students' ability and achievement validly using appropriate and varied instruments and procedures that accurately reflect what students do know (not just what they don't know, e.g., mainstream language and culture).

6. Foster a positive interrelationship among students, their families, the community and school based on respect for the knowledge students bring with them to school. Tapping into community resources, participating in community events, and valuing the contributions of families and community strengthen this bond.

7. Motivate students to become active participants in their learning through reflection, goal setting, self-evaluation, questioning, using feedback, and tailoring their learning strategies.

8. Encourage students to think critically by teaching them strategies for analyzing and synthesizing information and for viewing situations from multiple perspectives.

9. Challenge students to strive for excellence as defined by their potential to learn, regardless of past history of failure.

10. Assist students in becoming socially and politically conscious so they can be contributing, responsible participants in school and society (National Center for Culturally Responsive Educational Systems (NCCRESt), 2010).

According to Lee, Menkart, and Okazawa-Rey (2002), "multicultural education should help students, parents, teachers and administrators understand and relate to the histories, cultures and languages of people different from themselves" (p. vii). And indeed it should. In this new millennium statistics on education tell us that even today, some schools are more segregated than prior to *Brown v. Board of Education of Topeka* (Tatum, 2008) and that segregated classrooms, although thought to be the province of the inner city, are also apparent in both suburban and rural schools. This segregation on either side of the equation neither serves nor prepares our students for the increasingly small world they have inherited.

I believe, along with Lee, Menkart, and Okazawa-Rey (2002), and Tatum (2008), that these factors are crucial in all schools, no matter where they are located. Leadership must be open to the notion of multiculturalism as an educational framework in which teachers and administrators educate students as well as themselves by becoming culturally responsive practitioners. Multiculturalism must be more, however, than just a stroll into the world of the "other." Educators must move beyond the heroes and holidays approach that trivializes ethnic cultures and does not get to the essence of multicultural education. In its objectives, multicultural education "must be transformative, that is, encourage academic excellence that embraces critical skills for progressive social change" (Lee, Menkart, & Okazawa-Rey, 2002, p. vii).

Lee, Menkart, and Okazawa-Rey (2002) further asserted that in order for transformation to occur multicultural education must:

- Instill the importance of academic excellence;
- Examine the history and underlying causes of racism and its institutional features;
- Teach the connections between racism and other forms of inequality;
- Analyze the ways in which schools and education, as an institution of our society, have helped to support and perpetuate racism;
- Teach how racism hurts both peoples of color and White people, and prevents us from being effective allies;
- Show how White people and peoples of color throughout history have indeed worked together, and celebrate those efforts;
- Provide opportunities to collectively envision just and fair schools, communities and the larger society; and
- Inspire and empower us to do the necessary work to make those visions come true. (p. vii)

In addition to embracing a multicultural school framework, as recommended by many researchers, educators need institutional support in acquiring the tools and skills to be effective, culturally responsive educators. Culturally responsive pedagogic practice according to Chartock (2010) requires that educators engage in teaching and acting in ways that are in accordance with multicultural awareness, acceptance, appreciation, and action (p. x). To take that a step further, antiracist identity and cultural competence are attributes that are central to multicultural education and culturally responsive pedagogic practice.

Cultural competence encompasses sensitivity to cultures different from one's own, especially nondominant cultures. I believe the majority of educators have their hearts in the right place when they seek access to the profession. In my work with pre-service teachers I bear witness to the enthusiasm and motivation. I have seen these teachers work tirelessly with the best of intentions to help students who may come to school facing obstacles and issues not encountered by others, such as language barriers, social class, and racial status. I have seen the best of intentions backfire, through cultural misunderstandings, stereotype threats, and racial micro aggressions. Today, as we are in the second decade of the new millennium, we should hold ourselves, as educators in these environments, to the very ideals, standards, and expectations that we hold for our students. We no longer have the time to let the ball drop. The futures of our students and those not yet inhabiting America's twenty-first-century classrooms deserve more than just good intentions.

Deprogramming: Ruby Payne

I have returned to the topic of Ruby Payne and her framework for understanding poverty, which I discussed in Chapter One. Here, I am going to discuss further why I am concerned about the way the state of Vermont has embraced Ruby Payne's views on what she refers to as a "culture of poverty," since, at the same time, she perpetuates racist as well as classist stereotypes to unknowing, unconscious people, who may hold the best of intentions. Social workers, educators, and others in the nonprofit world have been walked down the Payne gauntlet. If you want to see power as well as privilege entrenched, try talking to White liberals about the obvious problems with Ruby Payne's framework for understanding poverty. It is like talking to a brick wall. I have tried on numerous occasions, along with other activists, to bring to light the problems with her flawed ideologies, but to no avail. Many, including the well intended, hold deeply defensive positions when concern is raised about her conservative, classist, and racist viewpoint. I have brought her up as a topic in many venues. Still, all I get is a headshake, and then it is back to the business of upholding the status quo. "It is not about race, but class" is a statement I often hear when attending to business in which equity is the topic of discussion. I realize however that many of us have been affected by the stigma that class creates when living in a society that bases a person's worth on their place in the social and racial hierarchies. Social class and status have a profound influence on how people view themselves and each other.

I believe Ruby Payne has had a deep hold on confusing and confounding the thinking of those who truly want to effect change but do not have the life experience, analytical lens, or tools to do the analysis other than through the frame of reference in which they have been socialized. Payne has a strong hold on the psyche of American middle-class, White, liberal teachers, with her Jeffersonian mythmaking—the assumption of the innate flaws held by people in poverty and the articulation of their presumed inferiority. This, along with dissemination of stereotyped misinformation, creates a big interruption for educators and others, preventing them from understanding that racism is alive and well, and that color blindness and cultural incompetence are factors that undermine the achievement of students regardless of class. The result is the proliferation of flawed perceptions and assumptions, further interrupting the conversation, and thus impeding the progress that might be attained in terms of reducing the achievement gap for both poor and minority students.

Because Ruby Payne has sustained such a deep hold on the way poverty is both explored and discussed in this state, there is much work to be done in undoing the mis-education that the human service community has invested in, in trying to grapple with issues of poverty in Vermont. Unfortunately, Ruby Payne has further confused and confounded many who serve populations in public institutions such as schools and social service agencies and who have bought into this paradigm. How do we deprogram the stereotypes and assumptions put forth by Payne's work? How do we support folks in the human services and education fields, enabling them to look at social class and poverty through a social justice lens? When will we look at the true roots and origins of poverty, examining it through the lens of capitalism and the global exploitation of peoples of color and of low social class? Until we once again have a clear understanding of history, capitalism, and its effects on people, we will continue to spin our wheels for equity to no avail.

Poverty and race should no longer be considered as qualifiers for poor outcomes for any student. It is up to those in positions of leadership to move the process forward by investing in their own development as leaders vested in transforming their schools to meet the educational, spiritual, and social-emotional needs of all students. We are now moving forward in that process. As stated earlier we have a district moving forward in its school transformation process, investing in becoming antiracist, multicultural, and culturally competent. I ask these important questions: How do we accomplish the work, when we have folks in our institutions that have been reinforced in their negative views on race and poverty through the work of Ruby Payne? How do we deprogram and countervail all of the education that our teachers and leaders have been involved in over the years that has elevated Ruby Payne to the status of expert for understanding poverty here in Vermont? I ask these questions because I know from talking to the male participants in this project that race was an issue in all of their lives at one time or another during their tenure in Vermont's public schools regardless of their social class.

As a social scientist and observer, my interest is in the power of the qualitative narrative as a source of primary data. I believe that bearing witness through testimony gives sound manifestation to the subjugated and concealed voices that can get to the heart of the issues affecting marginalized populations in America's schools. How can we create environments that are culturally responsive to students from the non-dominant culture?

According to the research, African American boys in America who attend public school have diminished chances of achievement and success compared to their White peers. Why can't it happen here? It has already, as a matter of fact. All too often, the study participants' experiences were formed by a variety of negative incidents, unjust discipline practices, and low teacher expectations such as stereotype threats, belief in their criminality, and bullying and harassment by not only students but teachers and administrators as well.

This information should not be misunderstood. I am not implying that all Black males have the same experiences in their schooling. Such a stance would be unrealistic. Nonetheless, it is no news that the dropout rates for Black and Latino males across the nation are at epic proportions because of many of the factors that contribute to dropping out.

This trend has been evident since the start of the new millennium, and the research points to a variety of systemic factors.

Hence, the research informs us that there is a distinct connection between discipline policy and practice (Ferguson, 2001; Reyes, 2006), special education (Kunjufu, 2005), and teacher attitudes and expectations (Delpit, 1995; Gay, 2010; Hallinan, 2008; Monroe, 2005), all of which relate to the success and meaningful school experience of Black youths and their ultimate achievement. I will not negate the influence that some factors outside the school have on outcomes. Such factors as poverty, under resourced schools, and/or violence in their neighborhoods are normally out of students' control. I also will not discount the importance of parental or guardian involvement, which is also influenced by how thoughtful, welcoming, and inclusive the school system is to families. But that is not the focus of this project. The focus is on experience from primary sources, former students themselves.

What I found most intriguing about the personal perspectives of the thirteen participants was that, even though all but one of them made it to graduation, their journeys were at times precarious, to say the least. Quite often there were barriers that could have caused them to disengage or possibly even drop out. For instance, spending the last year of one's high school in isolation, away from one's peers is a form of punitive punishment just short of incarceration. I find it remarkable that the participants spoke candidly and openly about their experiences, considering that no one up until now had been interested in finding out their point of view.

The primary purpose for this text is to provide a vehicle for those perspectives, by bringing to light the public school experiences of young Black men in Vermont. The stories serve as a guide for both pedagogic practice and policy making on a school-wide level in order to promote more equitable educational outcomes for all students. The analysis of the data indicates that some African American males who have attended public school in Vermont have had experiences that resemble those of their peers across the nation. Their input speaks to whom they are, both as individuals and as members of a group marginalized by racial history and status. I was witness to courage and strength as well as a willingness to overcome the systemic borders and barriers that exist in public schools. What I observed throughout the process were men who learned in what must have been sometimes difficult situations. These men are incredibly strong human beings. Their stories speak to their resistance, resilience, and tenacity in a system that is wrought with misperceptions and assumptions about them.

I initially started out wanting to know: How did African American or Black males perceive their own schooling experiences in Vermont public schools? How did they perceive those experiences in terms of discipline, climate, peer and teacher relationships, and support within the school? From the data analysis, the majority of participants expressed a variety of feelings around their educational experiences in relation to the domains addressed in the data. This resulting information is intended to send a clear message to all in the educational community that it is time to make a place at the table, for all of Vermont's new faces.

Field Notes: More Insights From the Field

"Prepare us with the tools and skills we need for the competitive life of college and career that awaits us after high school. Tell us about programs other than special education that offer alternatives to college, such as entrepreneurship opportunities that link life to learning." (Field notes)

After all the interviews were completed and the questions were asked, answered, and analyzed, I posed what I thought to be a very valuable question to the project participants. I asked them, as students who have already made the journey through school here in the Green Mountain State, "If you could envision an ideal school, what would it look like?" The responses were thoughtful, relevant, and deeply insightful.

Teacher expectation

One thing that came up in a majority of our conversations was the lack of teachers that reflected the students' cultures and race. Many felt that even though they had seen a huge gap in the lack of teachers of color, what was most important to them was that teachers respected them as individuals who also had hopes, dreams, and aspirations like their White peers. They also felt that teachers did not take them seriously.

One student complained about teachers who used students' academic challenges against them in the classroom. One talked about being made an example of with regard to the issue of not having homework by being shamed in front of his peers. Another talked about witnessing a less fluent reader being shamed by being made to read in front of the class while some students made fun of him. Nonetheless, those experiences aside, they hope that teachers as well as students see the Black males in the schools in their multiple identities, rather than simply adopting the socialized assumptions that the greater society holds for them as a raced group.

The need for male counselors

The research tells us that 85% of teachers are middle-class White women who come from working-class backgrounds. Historically, the relationship between Black males and White women has been fraught with dysfunction. Today the remnants of that dysfunctional relationship play out in schools. The levels of disconnect between males of color and White females is having a disastrous effect on Black males' achievement and success in school. The green book, *Racial Harassment in Vermont Public Schools* (Vermont Advisory Committee to the United States Commission on Civil Rights, 1999) outlined complaints by both students and their parents about teachers' negative perception of Black males as criminals.

The history of Black criminality goes back to the 1700s when the concept of a defective pathology assigned to free Blacks was used as a means to keep them on the margins of society (McIntyre, 1993). Having male teachers, even if they are White males, available for young men of color helps to reduce the cultural misunderstanding that has existed between Black men and White women for many centuries in America. Perhaps assuming the role of a culturally responsive educator can offer opportunities for White female teachers to investigate their perceptions of the "other." They will need to examine their own socialization by many of the standard tools within the society. Also, White teachers have to be informed about the history of African Americans and the historical role that gender has assumed due to the institution of slavery and Jim Crow.

What coaches can do

In my discussions with the young men who were athletes in their respective schools, I learned that it is not uncommon to be seen as an object of competition. Some Vermont schools are well known for their excellence in sports and for their student athletes. The journey of the Black athlete here has been a double-edged coin. First-generation, college-bound hopefuls may not know the protocols and procedures for taking the next step in their education post secondary school. However, in my eyes an effective teacher and coach should hold the expectation of their athlete succeeding academically, not just wish these young men to excel on the playing field in order to fill up the trophy case in the school lobby.

Preparation for life after high school, whether it is continuing education or work, was another response that came up during our talks. The participants in this project felt they needed more opportunities to explore their options for both work and college. Many found their way and got on track post high school.

Curriculum

African American history was mentioned as a subject that should be taught. In some of the conversations a few of the young men talked about schools that offered African American History as part of the curriculum. They said they would have been happy if they had that option when they attended their respective schools. They also said they learned a little about Africa during Western civilization class, and about African Americans during units on slavery and during Black History Month. As far as a course, they would love to see everybody have African and African American history in school.

The research informs us that traditional curriculum places the voice, perspective, values, and beliefs of the dominant culture at the center (Apple, 1995). The power of multicultural education and curriculum is that all voice in our pluralistic and diverse society is included. The rationale for this is that the student has the opportunity to discover our society and the world through the voices and lens of others, not just the dominator. By doing so the student is given the tools for critical thinking and the information they need to disrupt hegemony and the status quo. When students who are on the margins of the dominant paradigm do not see themselves in the curriculum it sends a clear message that they have no culture. No culture translates into low self-esteem and self-worth (Kunjufu, 2005).

Because I grew up at a time when Black identity was reclaimed in the late 1960s, my belief in a multicultural curriculum is influenced by the results of an Afrocentric curriculum made available to me in my high school in New York. I am the product of a school that taught us about ourselves during a challenging time of racial demographic shifts in our community. Let me share with you my story about how I learned to love history and myself.

In 1967 my parents, in search of better schools, moved the family to Long Island. The town we moved to had experienced rapid shifts in its racial demographic, with high percentages of racial integration in the schools occurring over a short period of time. Between 1967 and 1969, the year I graduated high school, my school went from being predominantly White to predominantly Black. It was clear that fear was the culprit, the catalyst that motivated people to flee town because they feared people who looked like me. Blockbusting and White flight were occurring right before my eyes. I was both confused and outraged. My salvation in the summer of 1968 was through staying connected to the school that became predominantly Black by working with high profile, successful Black people in the community. Both teachers and families worked diligently on building a school community that was caring, resourceful, and, most importantly, had our best interests at heart.

With the exodus of our town's White residents went many of the economic and social resources. It was the strength and vision of the community leadership, along with our families and the Black teachers at the schools, that helped us through this demographic change. In hindsight, I realize how hard and furiously they worked to build us up in order to keep us from the despair that racism causes (Dempsey & Noblit, 1996). Their due diligence on such a problematic issue gave me the will to investigate the human condition through the lens of the social observer. Moreover, during my junior year of high school I took an African Societies class, with Mrs. Carter. It was comforting to have a teacher who looked like me teach a course with the intention of building our self-esteem after what seemed to be a bad situation. What is most significant for me is that taking those courses in high school put me on the path to where and who I am today: a social scientist deeply invested in positive social change and racial justice.

Hence, when considering curriculum, please consider who is in the room when you choose curriculum with charged language like the N-word. Please prepare the class beforehand about the topic. Talk about how it is not the responsibility of students of color to explain these things to White kids. Remind those in the class not to ask individual Black people to speak for all people in the ethnic group.

In Gorski's (n.d.) "Seven Key Characteristics of a Multicultural Education Curriculum," it is said that content needs to be evaluated for charged language. I agree, and would advise all teachers to consider the factors that charged text might create in their classrooms. Here in Vermont, we have had a lot of charged texts delivered in classrooms, containing materials that reflect strong historical biases. In my interactions with lots of schools I have come across some fairly inexcusable behavior when the N-word has surfaced as a topic of discussion. I have even gotten an ample amount of pushback from primary school teachers who like to use the Mildred Taylor[4] series—a set of children's books marketed to primary grades and that are full of racial pejoratives. Can you imagine reading the N-word to second graders? As educators, teaching in an era of safe-school initiatives, we should also ask ourselves, how do books with such charged language (read as a class or as an individual) impact on concrete minds and on our interactions with difference in the classroom, hallway, or bus?

Field Notes: Summary

The most important step in providing males of color the opportunity to see the attainment of success, as an authentic possibility is for the community to become more informed and aware that race, culture, and identity matter. Once these factors are acknowledged the process of removing the blinders becomes more effective. By removing and erasing color blindness and by understanding just what the lawmakers meant we will take a step in the right direction in terms of gaining a historical framework for comprehending institutional inequities that are in the way of systemic change.

In order to even the playing field and decrease the achievement gap, we want teachers to move in the direction of becoming antiracist, anti-classist, and culturally responsive educators. The statistics continue to tell us that Black males are more likely to be involved in activities that are not conducive to their own success academically. The statistics also tell us that they are more likely than their White peers to be placed in special education classes, be suspended from school, gain the label of mentally retarded, or just drop out altogether. These are disturbing trends that tell us that Black boys are in crisis in our public school systems.

I believe, like many of my colleagues, that we can work together as a community of faculty, parents, administrators, policy makers, and stakeholders to reverse these trends. In reversing these trends, we need to create pathways for these young men to turn their lives around, as we have seen in the stories of some of the young men put before us.

The research available today on Black boys suggests that the following things are needed in order to overcome the dreadful outcomes males of color have been experiencing:

1. Strong school leadership who will take ownership of the work needed to get males on course for success.
2. Male empowerment sessions.
3. Culturally responsive schools (National Education Association (NEA), 2011, p. 2).

We are dealing with school systems that are irrelevant, archaic, and inadequate when it comes to meeting the needs of all students. Change certainly cannot happen in a vacuum. It has to be brought about in concert with the greater community. How do we as individuals initiate this process while waiting for others to come on board? We have some good examples in the states public schools.

I want to share a story about a former principal in a Vermont public school district who has turned the lives of some students around by leading through praxis. This principal led by example. Whenever I stepped into the school building, the leader pointed out the leadership of young students of color. This principal took great pride in the fact that these students overcome astounding odds in their journey as displaced people, new Americans, new Vermonters. She also highlighted the multiple languages they spoke while learning to master English. Some of the students already spoke four languages fluently. She did this by getting to know them, their families, and their stories. She no doubt expects great things from these wonderful human beings who are in her charge everyday. She never saw them as afflicted with a deficit, as criminals, or as incapable. She is an example of a leader guided by a moral compass to do the right thing for all students. Principals like this one are truly needed yet rare in order to facilitate school transformation. I am not saying other examples like these do not exist across the state, I am sure they do. However, in my mind this is a clear example of what Kailin and other research speak to in the literature.

I wonder what the lives of these students would be like if they were treated as just invisible numbers, as statistics. This principal sees all of these students as leaders, not in the future, but right now. Students, who come to school speaking not only one or two languages, but are learning a third language in this new land are accorded respect. A few of these youth not only had leadership roles in the school and in their classrooms, but also within their own families. This principal sees and acknowledges that to be multilingual is a gift, not a burden. Our leaders of tomorrow are here, but we have to keep them connected to their sense of self by keeping them connected to their cultural history.

Dr. Kunjufu, with whom I am in agreement on issues of Black males and they're schooling, stated that Black male students are having identity issues and problems. Those identity issues have to do with the history of Black men and women in this country as well as with Black males not understanding who they are because of the history of exploitation and captivity of stolen Africans (Prescott, 1992).

White students as well as students of color are at a loss when the curriculum is void of the African American experience in terms of race and race relations. We have an opportunity before us to create a framework of school transformation with an intentional focus on social justice and equity as preferred outcomes for all students. Let us not be deceived again, as we were over thirteen years ago, by a lack of urgency in response to our schools and students of color. The voices are telling us that it is time to wake up from our color-blind slumber. The statistics are becoming available and what is becoming apparent counters all the stock stories about Vermont and its inclusive, friendly schools for students of color. The data say that we have no time to be divisive in our arguments on how students should be served. We all must put aside our narrow visions and open up to the possibilities that, through the praxis of equity and inclusion, all students—regardless of race, social class, ethnicity, ability, gender, sexual orientation, and religious belief—will benefit from being educated in an environment that values, celebrates with mindful intention, and truly embraces diversity.

Today's diverse classrooms clearly require that educators possess (and put into practice) the attitudes, dispositions, and behaviors that are culturally competent and responsive to the multiple cultural and social identities they will encounter. What does that mean in the context of new-millennium schools? First and foremost, all teachers must start by knowing who they are, in all of their social identities. White teachers especially will benefit from a deeper understanding of the privilege they hold as White people by investigating how Whiteness evolved as a social construction, and the resulting benefits of White privilege. In order to bring an end to racism they must begin to see themselves, as well as their students, as human beings in a world that has unwittingly and unconsciously assigned them raced identities.

Speaking from my own experience, I have always been aware of myself as a human being in a racialized world. My personal experience with Jim Crow racism when I was eleven years old really affirmed my awareness of institutionalized racism. In our household, race and racism were discussed. It was these early "awakenings" that called me to action in different ways and at different times, leading me on the path to become, an advocate for social justice.

Traveling to the South in 1962 was a pivotal point in my life. The South taught me a lot about overt racial bigotry and hate. I was just eleven years old traveling south with my family, going from New York to Florida to visit relatives. After a short stopover to visit with family in Virginia, we headed south, arriving in a Georgia town just after nightfall. Not fully understanding the extent of the Deep South's rage toward people like myself, I always wondered why my father, who drove on these journeys, always drove nonstop.

We still had a short way to go until we would arrive at our destination, outside St. Augustine, Florida, where my parents had reserved a room for the family to rest at a Black boarding house. A rather quick pit stop at a gas station that was not very friendly, appeared to be a hideous marker of de jure segregation. There was a bathroom with the word "colored" on the door. I was stunned. For the first time I had experienced firsthand what I had heard other family members talk about: racism. Having grown up in ethnically and racially mixed neighborhoods in Brooklyn, I would not tolerate this. White people were and are part of both my biological and my extended family. From that day forward I promised myself that I would not accept the conditions and definitions placed on me by others. I planned to challenge the foe head-on by becoming an activist for social justice. Living in Vermont has made the application of my advocacy skills useful.

In conclusion, we cannot overlook the history of racism in Vermont and in the schools. If we remain color blind to the fact that these issues are still with us, we will never be able to make equitable schools a reality. We will never be able to create culturally responsive spaces where all students and their families feel as though they belong. Schools must be envisioned as communities, as environments where all students can succeed with the support of a community of educators, parents, and stakeholders who will hold expectations that all of them, regardless of individual circumstances, in order for them to reach their highest human potential.

Solving the social issues that are barriers to success for students of color will not be possible until we see achievement not just through the lens of class but also race. Until then, populations of young people will never be justly served. We can no longer afford, as leaders and educators of millennial students, believe that we are in a world where race no longer matters. In all of our acts as educators we must first truly see in order to affirm our students' identities. Race is a salient part of identity, akin to social class and our other social identities. In America, where skin color holds such high capital, we have no choice but to see race as an enduring barrier to equity.

Perhaps, W. E. B. Du Bois was prescient: the problem with the twentieth century was the color line. It is likely that he would not be surprised, subtle as it is, that race still matters in the twenty-first century too.

Notes

1. For more on graduation rates, and Black males in Vermont, see Schott Foundation for Public Education (2010).
2. For more information on how graduation rates are formulated, see Alliance for Excellent Education (2008).
3. For more on the cost of racism to White identity development in White children, see Derman-Sparks & Ramsey (2006).
4. For more on Mildred Taylor and racialized language in young children's books, see Taylors works, *The Friendship* (1987), *Mississippi Bridge* (1990), and *The Well: David's Story* (1995).

Adams, C. (2008). What are your expectations? The challenge of teaching across race. Scholastic Instructor, 117(4), 26–30.

Allen, Q. (2010). Racial microaggressions: The schooling experiences of Black middle-class males in Arizona's secondary schools. Journal of African American Males in Education, 1(2), 125–143.

Alliance for Excellent Education. (2008). Understanding graduation rates. Retrieved from http//http://www.all4ed.org/publication_material/understanding_HSgradrates

Anderson, J. (1988). The education of Blacks in the South, 1860–1935, Chapel Hill, NC: University of North Carolina Press.

Anyon, J. (1981). Social class and school knowledge. Curriculum Inquiry, 11(1), 3–42.

Apple, M. W. (1995). Cultural capital and official knowledge. In M. Bérubé & C. Nelson (Eds.), Higher education under fire: Politics, economics, and the crisis of the humanities (pp. 91–107). New York, NY: Routledge.

Atwater, S. (2008). Waking up to difference: Teachers, color-blindness, and the effects on students of color. Journal of Instructional Psychology, 35(3), 246–253.

Banks, J. (2006). Race, culture and education: The selected works of James A. Banks. London, UK: Routledge.

Banks, J. (Ed.). (1996). Multicultural education, transformative knowledge, and action: Historical and contemporary perspectives. New York, NY: Teachers College Press.

Bell, D. (1992). Faces at the bottom of the well: The permanence of racism. New York, NY: Basic Books.

Bell, L. A. (2010). Storytelling for social justice: Connecting narrative and the arts in antiracist teaching. New York, NY: Routledge.

Berlin, I. (1998). Many thousands gone: The first two centuries of slavery in North America. Cambridge, MA: Harvard University Press.

Bireda, M. (2002). Eliminating racial profiling in school discipline: Cultures in conflict. Lanham, MD: Scarecrow Press.

Bissex, G. (1987). Year-long classroom-based studies. In G. Bissex & R. Bullock (Eds.), Seeing for ourselves: Case-study research by teachers of writing (pp. 31–45). Portsmouth, NH: Heinemann.

Blackmon, D. (2008). Slavery by another name: The re-enslavement of Black Americans from the Civil War to World War II. New York, NY: Doubleday.

Blumenson, E., & Nilsen, E. (2003). One strike and you're out? Constitutional constraints on zero tolerance in public education. Washington University Law Quarterly, 81(1), 65–117.

Bonilla-Silva, E. (2006). Racism without racists: Color-blind racism and the persistence of racial inequality in the United States (2nd ed.). Oxford, UK: Rowman & Littlefield.

Bourdieu, P. (1977). Cultural reproduction and social reproduction. In J. Karabel & A. H. Halsey (Eds.), Power and ideology in education (pp. 487–511). New York, NY: Oxford University Press.

Bowles, S. (1975). Unequal education and the reproduction of the social division of labor. In M. Carnoy (Ed.), Schooling in a corporate society: The political economy of education in America (2nd ed., pp. 47–53). New York, NY: McKay.

Bowles, S., & Gintis, H. (1976). Schooling in capitalist America: Educational reform and the contradictions of economic life. New York, NY: Basic Books.

Brady, K., Forton, M. B., & Porter, D. (2010). Rules in school: Teaching discipline in the responsive classroom. Turners Falls, MA: Northeast Foundation for Children.

Brown, M. C., & Bartee, R. (Eds.). (2009). The broken cisterns of African American education: Academic performance and achievement in the post-Brown era. Charlotte, NC: Information Age.

Burlington school district 2009–2010 annual report (2011, February). Retrieved from http://bsdweb.bsdvt.org/Board/annualreports/Feb2011.pdf

Carger, C. (2009). Dreams deferred: Dropping out and struggling forward. Charlotte, NC: Information Age.

Carter, D. (2008). Achievement as resistance: The development of a critical race achievement ideology among Black achievers. Harvard Educational Review, 78(3), 466–497.

Casella, R. (2003). Zero tolerance policy in schools: Rationale, consequences, and alternatives. Teachers College Record, 105(5), 872–892.

Charney, R. (1997). Teaching children to care: Management in the responsive classroom. Greenfield, MA: Northeast Foundation for Children.

Charney, R., Clayton, M. K., & Wood, C. (1997). The responsive classroom: Guidelines. Greenfield, MA: Northeast Foundation for Children.

Chartock, R. (2010). Strategies and lessons for culturally responsive teaching: A primer for K–12 teachers. Boston, MA: Pearson.

Cheney, K. B., & Vermont Advisory Committee. (1999). Racial harassment in Vermont public schools. Washington, DC: U.S. Commission on Civil Rights, Eastern Regional Office.

Chenoweth, K. (2007). It's being done: Academic success in unexpected schools. Cambridge, MA: Harvard Education Press.

Children's Defense Fund. (2007). America's cradle to prison pipeline: A Children's Defense Fund report. Washington, DC: Author. Retrieved from http://www.childrensdefense.org/child-research-data-publications/data/cradle-prison-pipeline-report-2007-full-lowres.pdf, and http://cdf.childrensdefense.org/site/DocServer/CPP_report_2007_summary.pdf?docID=6001

Clinton, W. J. (1995, October 16). The President's speech on race relations at The University of Texas. Retrieved from http://clinton1.nara.gov/White_House/EOP/OP/html/OP_Speeches.html, http://clinton1.nara.gov/White_House/EOP/OP/html/ut.html, and http://www.cnn.com/US/9510/megamarch/10-16/clinton/update/transcript.html

Connerley, M. L., & Pedersen, P. B. (2005). Leadership in a diverse and multicultural environment: Developing awareness, knowledge and skills. Thousand Oaks, CA: Sage.

Cremin, L. (1980) American education: The national experience, 1783–1876. New York, NY: Harper and Row.

Creswell, J. (1998). Qualitative inquiry and research design: Choosing among five traditions. Thousand Oaks, CA: Sage.

Davis, A. Y. (1997). Race and criminalization: Black Americans and the punishment industry. In W. Lubiano (Ed.), The house that race built: Black Americans, U.S. terrain (pp. 264–279). New York, NY: Anchor.

DeAngelis, T. (2009). Unmasking 'racial microaggressions.' American Psychological Association, 40(2), 42.

Delgado, R. (Ed). (1995). Critical race theory: The cutting edge. Philadelphia, PA: Temple University Press.

Delpit, L. (1995). Other people's children: Cultural conflict in the classroom. New York, NY: New Press.

Dempsey, V., & Noblit, G. (1996). Caring and continuity: The demise of caring in an African-American community, one consequence of school desegregation. In D. Eaker-Rich & J. Van Galen (Eds.), Caring in an unjust world: Negotiating borders and barriers in schools (pp. 113–128). Albany, NY: State University of New York Press.

Derman-Sparks, L., & Brunson Phillips, C. (1997). Teaching/learning anti-racism: A developmental approach. New York, NY: Teachers College Press.

Derman-Sparks, L., & Ramsey, P. (2006). What if all the children are White?: Anti-bias multicultural education with young children and families. New York, NY: Teachers College Press.

Dewey, J. (1959). Dewey on education: Selections. New York, NY: Teachers College.

Dewey, J. (2009). The school and society, & The child and the curriculum. Lexington, KY: Feather Trail Press.

Du Bois, W. E. B. (1973). The education of Black people: Ten critiques, 1906–1960 (H. Aptheker, Ed.). New York, NY: Monthly Review Press.

Du Bois, W. E. B. (1993). The souls of Black folk: Essays and sketches. New York, NY: Random House.

Dunbar, D. (2007). Leading and learning: A passion for justice (Unpublished essay).

Dunbar, D. (2009). Leading the conversation: In-service teachers' attitudes about students of color, anti-racism/cultural, professional development, and the need for purposeful dialogue on racism in Vermont public schools (Unpublished essay).

Ekstrom, R. B., Goertz, M. E., Pollack, J. M., & Rock, D. A. (1986). Who drops out of high school and why? Findings from a national study. Teachers College Record, 87(3), 356–373.

Elliot, A. J., and Devine, P. G. (1994). On the motivational nature of cognitive dissonance: Dissonance as psychological discomfort. *Journal of Personality and Social Psychology, 67*, 382-394.

Ember, C., Ember, M., & Peregrine, P. (2005). Anthropology (11th ed.). Upper Saddle River, NJ: Pearson/Prentice Hall.

Emerson, R., Fretz, R., & Shaw, L. (1995). Writing ethnographic fieldnotes. Chicago, IL: University of Chicago Press.

Epstein, J. L., Sanders, M. G., Sheldon, S. B., Simon, B. S., Salinas, K. C., Jansorn, N. R., et al. (2009). School, family, and community partnerships: Your handbook for action (3rd ed.). Thousand Oaks, CA: Corwin Press.

Fashola, O. (Ed.). (2005). Educating African American males: Voices from the field. Thousand Oaks, CA: Corwin Press.

Ferguson, A. (2001). Bad boys: Public schools in the making of Black masculinity. Ann Arbor, MI: University of Michigan Press.

Festinger, L. (1957). *A theory of cognitive dissonance*. Stanford, CA: Stanford University Press.

Fields, B. (2001). Presentation given at a "School" for the producers of RACE the Power of an Illusion, PBS—March 2001 edited transcript, http://www.pbs.org/race/000_About/002_04-background-02-02.htm

Fireside, H. (2004). Separate and unequal: Homer Plessy and the Supreme Court case that legalized racism. New York, NY: Carroll & Graf.

Ford, B. A. (1995). African American community involvement processes and special education: Essential networks for effective education. In B. A. Ford, F. E. Obiakor, & J. M. Patton (Eds.), Effective education of African American exceptional learners: New perspectives (pp. 235–272). Austin, TX: Pro-Ed.

Fuhrman, S. (2008). If we're talking about race, let's talk about education. Education Week, 27(36), 24.

Gabriel, T. (2010, November 9). Proficiency of Black students is found to be far lower than expected. The New York Times. Retrieved from http://www.nytimes.com/2010/11/09/education/09gap.html

Gallagher, N. L. (2001). Vermont eugenics: A documentary history. Retrieved from http://www.uvm.edu/~eugenics/

Gay, G. (2010). Culturally responsive teaching: Theory, research, and practice (2nd ed.). New York, NY: Teachers College Press.

Gibbs, G. (2007). Analyzing qualitative data. London, UK: Sage.

Glesne, C. (2006). Becoming qualitative researchers: An introduction (3rd ed.). Boston, MA: Pearson.

Gorski, P. (2008). Peddling poverty for profit: Elements of oppression in Ruby Payne's framework. Equity and Excellence in Education, 41(1), 130–148.

Gorski, P. (n.d.). Seven key characteristics of a multicultural education curriculum. EdChange and the Multicultual Pavilion. Retrieved from http://www.edchange.org/handouts.html and http://www.edchange .org/multicultural/resources/ct_characteristics.html

Gorski, P.(2009). Cognitive dissonance: A critical tool in social justice teaching. White paper, www.edchange.org/publications/cognitive-dissonance.pdf

Greene, J., Pranis, K., & Ziedenberg, J., (2006). Disparity by design: How drug-free zone laws impact racial disparity—and fail to protect youth. Washington, DC: Justice Policy Institute.

Hall, H. (2006). Mentoring young men of color: Meeting the needs of African American and Latino students. Oxford, UK: Rowman & Littlefield.

Hall, J. N., & Parker, L. (2007). Rethinking No Child Left Behind using critical race theory. In C. Sleeter (Ed.), Facing accountability in education: Democracy and equity at risk (pp. 132–144). New York, NY: Teachers College Press.

Hallinan, M. T. (2001). Sociological perspectives on Black-White inequalities in American schooling. Sociology of Education, 74 (Extra Issue), 50–70.

Hallinan, M. (2008). Teacher influences on students' attachment to school. Sociology of Education, 81(3), 271–283.

Hancock, S. (2006.) White women's work: On the front lines of urban education. In J. Landsman & C. W. Lewis (Eds.), White teachers/diverse classrooms: A guide to building inclusive schools, promoting high expectations, and eliminating racism (pp. 93–109). Sterling, VA: Stylus.

Hanisch, C. (1970). The personal is political. In S. Firestone & A. Koedt (Eds.), Notes from the second year: Women's liberation (pp. 76–78). Retrieved from http://www.carolhanisch.org/CHwritings/PIP.html

Heck, R. (2004). Studying educational and social policy: Theoretical concepts and research methods. New York, NY: Routledge.

Herbert, B. (2007, April 9). 6-year-olds under arrest. The New York Times, p. A17. Retrieved from http://www.nytimes.com/2007/04/09/opinion/09herbert.html?scp=1&sq=herbert%20+%202007%20+%20%22six%20year%20old%22&st=cse

Herrnstein, R., & Murray, C. (1994). The bell curve: Intelligence and class structure in American life. New York, NY: Free Press.

Higginbotham, A. L., Jr. (1978). In the matter of color: Race and the American legal process: The colonial period. New York, NY: Oxford University Press.

Hilliard, A. G. (1998). What do we need to know now? "Race," identity, hegemony, and education. Speech given at the conference on Race, Research and Education. Chicago, IL: Chicago Urban League and the Spencer Foundation. Retrieved from http://www.africawithin.com/hilliard/what_now.htm

Hirsch, E. D., Jr. (2001). The roots of the education wars. In T. Loveless (Ed.), The great curriculum debate. Washington, DC: Brookings Institution Press. Retrieved from Catholic Education Resource Center (CERC), http://catholiceducation.org/articles/education/ed0174.html

Homan, R. (1991). The ethics of social research. New York, NY: Longman.

Horton, J. O., & Horton, L. E. (2005). Slavery and the making of America. New York, NY: Oxford University Press.

Irvine, J. J. (1990). Black students and school failure: Policies, practices, and prescriptions. New York, NY: Greenwood Press.

Irving, M. (2006). Practicing what we teach: Experiences with reflective practice and critical engagement. In J. Landsman & C. W. Lewis (Eds.), White teachers/diverse classrooms: A guide to building inclusive schools, promoting high expectations, and eliminating racism (pp. 195–202). Sterling, VA: Stylus.

Jefferson, T. (1982). Notes on the State of Virginia (William Peden, Ed.). Chapel Hill, NC: University of North Carolina Press.

John Dewey. (2012). Encyclopaedia Britannica. Retrieved from http://www.britannica.com/EBchecked/topic/160445/John-Dewey

Jones, S. (Ed.). (2009). The state of Black America, 2009: Message to the President. New York, NY: National Urban League.

Justice Policy Institute. (2005, October 3). Factsheet: Crime, race and juvenile justice policy in perspective. Retrieved from http://www.justicepolicy.org/research/2047

Kailin, J. (1999). How White teachers perceive the problem of racism in their schools: A case study in 'liberal' Lakeview. Teachers College Record, 100(4), 724–750.

Katzenstein, M. F., & Reppy, J. (Eds.). (1999). Beyond zero tolerance: Discrimination in military culture. Lanham, MD: Rowman & Littlefield.

Kennedy, R. (1997). Race, crime, and the law. New York, NY: Pantheon Books.

Kozol, J. (2005). The shame of the nation: The restoration of apartheid schooling in America. New York, NY: Three Rivers Press.

Kunjufu, J. (2005). Countering the conspiracy to destroy Black boys (2nd ed.). Chicago, IL: African American Images.

Ladson-Billings, G. (1994). The dreamkeepers: Successful teachers of African American children. San Francisco, CA: Jossey-Bass.

Ladson-Billings, G., & Tate, W., IV. (1995). Toward a critical race theory of education. Teachers College Record, 97(1), 47–68.

Landsman, J., & Lewis, C. W. (Eds.). (2006). White teachers/diverse classrooms: A guide to building inclusive schools, promoting high expectations, and eliminating racism. Sterling, VA: Stylus.

Lee, E., Menkart, D., & Okazawa-Rey, M. (2002). Introduction. In E. Lee, D. Menkart, & M. Okazawa-Rey (Eds.), Beyond heroes and holidays: A practical guide to K–12 anti-racist, multicultural education and staff development (2nd ed., pp. vii–xiii). Washington, DC: Teaching for Change.

Loewen, J. (2005). Sundown towns: A hidden dimension of American racism. New York, NY: Touchstone.

Losen, D., & Skiba, R. (2010). Suspended education: Urban middle schools in crisis. Southern Poverty Law Center. Retrieved from www.southernpovertylawcenter.org, http://www.splcenter.org/sites/default/files/downloads/publication/Suspended_Education.pdf, and http://www.splcenter.org/get-informed/publications/suspended-education

MacLeod, J. (1987). Ain't no makin' it: Aspirations and attainment in a low-income neighborhood. Boulder: Westview Press Inc.

Marx, S. (2006). Revealing the invisible: Confronting passive racism in teacher education. New York, NY: Routledge.

Mauer, M., King, R. S., & Young, M. C. (2004, May). The meaning of 'life': Long prison sentences in context. Washington, DC: The Sentencing Project. Retrieved from http://www.sentencingproject.org/doc/publications/inc_meaningoflife.pdf

Maxwell, J. A. (2005). Qualitative research design: An interactive approach (2nd ed.). Thousand Oaks, CA: Sage.

McIntosh, P. (2000). White privilege: Unpacking the invisible knapsack. In J. Noel (Ed.), Sources: Notable selections in multicultural education (pp. 115–120). Guilford, CT: Dushkin/McGraw-Hill.

McIntyre, C. C. L. (1993). Criminalizing a race: Free Blacks during slavery. Queens, NY: Kayode.

McWhorter, J. H. (2000). Losing the race: Self sabotage in Black America. New York, NY: Simon & Schuster.

Mears, C. (2009). Interviewing for education and social science research: The gateway approach. New York, NY: Palgrave Macmillan.

Middleton, V., Coleman, K., & Lewis, C. W. (2006). Black/African American families: Coming of age in predominately White communities. In J. Landsman & C. W. Lewis (Eds.), White teachers/diverse classrooms: A guide to building inclusive schools, promoting high expectations, and eliminating racism (pp. 162–182). Sterling, VA: Stylus.

Miller, A. (1990). For your own good: Hidden cruelty in child-rearing and the roots of violence (3rd ed.). New York, NY: Farrar, Strauss & Giroux.

Milner, H. (2006). But good intentions are not enough: Theoretical and philosophical relevance in teaching students of color. In J. Landsman & C. W. Lewis (Eds.), White teachers/diverse classrooms: A guide to building inclusive schools, promoting high expectations, and eliminating racism (pp. 79–90). Sterling, VA: Stylus.

Monroe, C. R. (2005). Why are 'bad boys' always Black? Causes of disproportionality in school discipline and recommendations for change. Clearing House, 79(1), 45–50.

Murrell, P., Jr. (2002). African-centered pedagogy: Developing schools of achievement for African American children. Albany, NY: State University of New York Press.

National Center for Culturally Responsive Educational Systems (NCCRESt). http://www.NCCRES.org

National Education Association (NEA). (2010, March). Status of the American public school teacher 2005–2006. Retrieved from http://www.nea.org/assets/docs/HE/2005-06StatusTextand AppendixA.pdf

National Education Association (NEA). (2011, February). Race against time: Educating Black boys. Retrieved from http://www.nea.org/assets/docs/educatingblackboys11rev.pdf

Neill, M. (1989). Fiery crosses in the green mountains: The story of the Ku Klux Klan in Vermont. Randolph Center, VT: Greenhills Books.

New England Common Assessment Program (NECAP). (2011). Retrieved from http://education.vermont.gov/new/html/pgm_assessment/necap.html

Nieto, S. (2000). Affirming diversity: The sociopolitical context of multicultural education (3rd ed.). New York, NY: Longman.

No Child Left Behind, from the Executive Summary of No Child Left Behind (January 8, 2002). (2009). In C. Kridel (Ed.), Education: Classic edition sources (4th ed., pp. 180–184). Boston, MA: McGraw-Hill.

Noddings, N. (1984). Caring: A feminine approach to ethics and moral education. Berkeley, CA: University of California Press.

Noddings, N. (2007). When school reform goes wrong. New York, NY: Teachers College Press.

Noguera, P. A. (2003). The trouble with black boys: The role and influence of environmental and cultural factors on the academic performance of African American males. Urban Education, 38(4), 431–459.

Noguera, P. (2008). The trouble with Black boys: And other reflections on race, equity, and the future of public education. San Francisco, CA: Jossey-Bass.

Noguera, P., & Wing, J. Y. (2006). Unfinished business: Closing the racial achievement gap in our schools. San Francisco, CA: Jossey-Bass.

Novak, J. D., & Gowin, D. B. (1984). Learning how to learn. Cambridge, UK: Cambridge University Press.

Nurse, A. (2010). Locked up, locked out: Young men in the juvenile justice system. Nashville, TN: Vanderbilt University Press.

Oakes, J., & Lipton, M. (2007). Teaching to change the world (3rd ed.). Boston, MA: McGraw-Hill.

Obama, B. (2008, March 18). A more perfect union. National Constitution Center. Retrieved from http://www.constitutioncenter.org/amore perfectunion/ and http://www.latimes.com/news/nationworld/ nation/la-na-campaign19mar19-speech,0,3568071.story

Ogbu, J. U. (1978). Minority education and caste: The American system in a cross-cultural perspective. New York: Academic Press.

Ogbu, J. U. (1987). Variability in minority school performance: A problem in search of an explanation. Anthropology & Education Quarterly, 18(4), 312–334.

Ogbu, J. U. (1992). Adaptation to minority status and impact on school success. Theory Into Practice, 31(4), 287–295.

Omi, M., & Winant, H. (1994). Racial formation in the United States: From the 1960s to the 1990s (2nd ed.). New York, NY: Routledge.

Patton, M. (2002). Qualitative research and evaluation methods (3rd ed.). Thousand Oaks, CA: Sage.

Payne, R. (1996). A framework for understanding poverty (4th rev. ed.). Highlands, TX: aha! Process.

Payne, R., DeVol, P., & Dreussi Smith, T. (2001). Bridges out of poverty: Strategies for professionals and communities. Highlands, TX: aha! Process.

Pitre, A., Pitre, E., Ray, R. & Hilton-Pitre, T. (2009). Educating African American students: Foundations, curriculum, and experiences. Lanham, MD: Rowman & Littlefield.

Plessy v. Ferguson, 163 U.S. 537 (1896). U.S. Supreme Court. Retrieved from http://caselaw.lp.findlaw.com/scripts/getcase.pl?court=us& vol=163&invol=537

Polite, V. C., & Davis, J. E. (Eds.). (1999). African American males in school and society: Practices and policies for effective education. New York, NY: Teachers College Press.

Portner, J. (1996, October 23). Suspensions spur debate over discipline codes. Education Week, 16(8), 10.

Prescott, F. (1992). SETCLAE: Self-esteem through culture leads to academic excellence. Chicago, IL: African American Images.

Price, J. (2000). Against the odds: The meaning of school and relationships in the lives of six African-American men. Stamford, CT: Ablex.

Price, V. C. (2006). I don't understand why my African American students are not achieving: An exploration of the connection among personal power, teacher perceptions, and the academic engagement of African American students. In J. Landsman & C. W. Lewis (Eds.), White teachers, diverse classrooms: A guide to building inclusive schools, promoting high expectations, and eliminating racism (pp. 122–136). Sterling, VA: Stylus.

Pulliam, J., & Van Patten, J. (1999). History of education in America (7th ed.). Upper Saddle River, NJ: Prentice Hall.

Reyes, A. (2006). Discipline, achievement, and race: Is zero tolerance the answer? Lanham, MD: Rowman & Littlefield.

Rothenberg, P. (2005). White privilege: Essential readings on the other side of racism (2nd ed.). New York, NY: Worth.

Sadovnik, A. (1991). Basil Bernstein's theory of pedagogic practice: A structuralist approach. Sociology of Education, 64(1), 48–63.

Schott Foundation for Public Education. (2010). Yes we can: The Schott 50 state report on public education and Black males. Cambridge, MA: Author. Retrieved from http://blackboysreport.org/bbreport.pdf

Seidman, I. (2006). Interviewing as qualitative research: A guide for researchers in education and the social sciences (3rd ed.). New York, NY: Teachers College Press.

Singleton, G. E., & Linton, C. (2006). Courageous conversations about race: A field guide for achieving equity in schools. Thousand Oaks, CA: Corwin Press.

Skiba, R. J., & Rausch, M. K. (2006). Zero tolerance, suspension, and expulsion: Questions of equity and effectiveness. In C. M. Evertson & C. S. Weinstein (Eds.), Handbook of classroom management: Research, practice, and contemporary issues (pp. 1063–1089). Mahwah, NJ: Lawrence Erlbaum.

Sleeter, C. (Ed.). (2007). Facing accountability in education: Democracy and equity at risk. New York, NY: Teachers College Press.

Smedley, A. (1999). Race in North America: Origin and evolution of a worldview. Boulder, CO: Westview Press.

Smith, H. (2009). The questions before us: Opportunity, education and equity. In S. Jones (Ed.), The state of Black America, 2009: Message to the President (pp. 45–55). New York, NY: National Urban League.

Solomon, R. P. (1992). Black resistance in high school: Forging a separatist culture. Albany,NY: State University of New York Press.

Solorzano, D. (1997). Images and words that wound: Critical race theory, racial stereotyping, and teacher education. Teacher Education Quarterly, 24(3), 5–19.

Spring, J. (2005). The American school, 1642–2004 (6th ed.). Boston, MA: McGraw-Hill.

Spring, J. (2008). The American school: From the puritans to No Child Left Behind (7th ed.). Boston, MA: McGraw-Hill.

Stack, C. B. (1975). All our kin: Strategies for survival in a Black community. New York, NY: Harper & Row.

Spring, J. (2010). Deculturalization and the struggle for equality: A brief history of the education of dominated cultures in the United States (4th ed.). Boston, MA: McGraw-Hill.

Stake, R. (1995). The art of case study research. Thousand Oaks, CA: Sage.

Steel, C. M., Spencer, S. J., & Aronson, J. (1995). Stereotype threat and the intellectual test performance of African Americans. Journal of Personality and Social Psychology, 69 (5), 797–811

Steel, C. M., Spencer, S. J., & Aronson, J. (2002). Contending with group image: The psychology of stereotype and social identity threat. In M. Zanna (Ed.), Advances in experimental social psychology (Vol. 34, pp. 379–440). New York, NY: Academic Press.

Sue, D. W. (2004). Whiteness and ethnocentric monoculturalism: Making the "Invisible" Visible. American Psychologist, 59(8), 759-769.

Sue, D. W. (2010). Microaggressions in everyday life: Race, gender, and sexual orientation. Hoboken, NJ: Wiley.

Sue, D. W., Capodilupo, C. M., Torino, G. C., Bucceri, J. C., Holder, A. M. B., Nadal, K. L., et al. (2007). Racial microaggressions in everyday life: Implications for clinical practice. American Psychologist, 62(4), 271–286.

Sue, D. W., Lin, A. I., Torino, G. C., Capodilupo, C. M., & Rivera, D. P. (2009). Racial microaggressions and difficult dialogues on race in the classroom. Cultural Diversity and Ethnic Minority Psychology, 15(2), 183–190.

Tarkan, L. (2002, November 19). Educating schools about life with asthma. The New York Times. Retrieved from http://www.nytimes.com/2002/11/19/health/educating-schools-about-life-with-asthma.html?scp=1&sq=%22Educating%20schools%20about%20life%20with%20asthma%22&st=cse

Task force report on the recommended strategic plan for diversity, equity, and inclusion for the Burlington school district. (2011, October). Retrieved from http://www.bsdvt.org/diversity/taskforce/BSD_Task_Force_Report_2011.pdf

Tatum, B. (2008). Can we talk about race?: And other conversations in an era of school resegregation. Boston, MA: Beacon Press.

Taylor, M. (1987). The friendship. New York, NY: Dial Books.

Taylor, M. (1990). Mississippi bridge. New York, NY: Dial Books.

Taylor, M. (1995). The well: David's story. New York, NY: Dial Books.

Teel, K., & Obidah, J. (2008). Building racial and cultural competence in the classroom: Strategies from urban educators. New York, NY: Teachers College Press.

Thousand, J. S., & Villa, R. A. (1995). Inclusion: Alive and well in the green mountain state. Phi Delta Kappan, 77(4), 288–291.

Tompkins, J. (1996). A life in school: What the teacher learned. New York, NY: Perseus Books.

United Nations. (1989). Convention on the rights of the child. Retrieved from http://www2.ohchr.org/english/law/crc.htm

United States Census Bureau. (2010). American community survey: Vermont. Retrieved from http://factfinder.census.gov/

United States Department of Education. (2009, September). High school dropout and completion rates in the United States: 2007: Compendium report. Retrieved from http://nces.ed.gov/pubs2009/2009064.pdf

Vaught, S., & Castagno, A. (2008). 'I don't think I'm a racist': Critical race theory, teacher attitudes, and structural racism. Race, Ethnicity and Education, 11(2), 95–113.

Vermont Advisory Committee to the United States Commission on Civil Rights. (1999). Racial harassment in Vermont public schools.

Washington, DC: U.S. Commission on Civil Rights, Eastern Regional Office.

Vermont Advisory Committee to the United States Commission on Civil Rights. (2003). Racial harassment in Vermont public schools: A progress report. Washington, DC: U.S. Commission on Civil Rights, Eastern Regional Office.

Vermont Department of Education. (2010, July). Vermont public school dropout and high school completion report: For the 2008–2009 school year. Retrieved from http://education.vermont.gov/new/pdfdoc/data/dropout/educ_data_dropout_completion_09_rev.pdf

Vermont Department of Health. (2009). 2009 youth risk behavior survey. Retrieved from http://healthvermont.gov/pubs/yrbs2009/documents/YRBS_2009.pdf

Vinovskis, M. (2009). From a nation at risk to No Child Left Behind: National education goals and the creation of federal education policy. New York, NY: Teachers College Press.

Walker, V. S., & Archung, K. N. (2003). The segregated schooling of Blacks in the southern United States and South Africa. Comparative Education Review (Special issue on Black populations globally), 47(1), 21–40.

Walker, V. S., & Snarey, J. (2004). Race-ing moral formation: African American perspectives on care and justice. New York, NY: Teachers College Press.

Walker-Dalhouse, D. (2005). Discipline: Responding to socioeconomic and racial differences. Childhood Education, 82(1), 24–29.

Watkins, W. (2001). The White architects of Black education: Ideology and power in America, 1865–1954. New York, NY: Teachers College Press.

Watkins, W., Lewis, J., & Chou, V. (2001). Race and education: The roles of history and society in educating African American students. Boston, MA: Allyn & Bacon.

Weis, L., & Fine, M. (2005). Beyond silenced voices: Class, race, and gender in United States schools (Rev. ed.). Albany, NY: State University of New York Press.

William, K. (2007). The spirit of the griot. Rethinking Schools, 22(1), 13. Retrieved from http://www.rethinkingschools.org/archive/22_01/need221.shtml

Williams, H. (2005). Self-taught: African American education in slavery and freedom. Chapel Hill, NC: University of North Carolina Press.

Williams, P. (1998.) Seeing a color-blind future: The paradox of race. New York, NY: Noonday Press.

Willis, P. (1977). Learning to labor: How working class kids get working class jobs. New York, NY: Columbia University Press.

Wolcott, H. (2009). Writing up qualitative research (3rd ed.). Thousand Oaks, CA: Sage.

Woodson, C. G. (1990). The mis-education of the Negro. Trenton, NJ: Africa World Press.

Wright, R., & Decker, S. (1997). Armed robbers in action: Stickups and street culture. Boston, MA: Northeastern University Press.

INDEX

ROCHELLE BROCK &
RICHARD GREGGORY JOHNSON III,
Executive Editors

Black Studies and Critical Thinking is an interdisciplinary series which examines the intellectual traditions of and cultural contributions made by people of African descent throughout the world. Whether it is in literature, art, music, science, or academics, these contributions are vast and far-reaching. As we work to stretch the boundaries of knowledge and understanding of issues critical to the Black experience, this series offers a unique opportunity to study the social, economic, and political forces that have shaped the historic experience of Black America, and that continue to determine our future. Black Studies and Critical Thinking is positioned at the forefront of research on the Black experience, and is the source for dynamic, innovative, and creative exploration of the most vital issues facing African Americans. The series invites contributions from all disciplines but is specially suited for cultural studies, anthropology, history, sociology, literature, art, and music.

Subjects of interest include (but are not limited to):

- EDUCATION
- SOCIOLOGY
- HISTORY
- MEDIA/COMMUNICATION
- RELIGION/THEOLOGY
- WOMEN'S STUDIES

- POLICY STUDIES
- ADVERTISING
- AFRICAN AMERICAN STUDIES
- POLITICAL SCIENCE
- LGBT STUDIES

For additional information about this series or for the submission of manuscripts, please contact Dr. Brock (Indiana University Northwest) at brock2@iun.edu or Dr. Johnson (University of San Francisco) at rgjohnsoniii@usfca.edu.

To order other books in this series, please contact our Customer Service Department:

(800) 770-LANG (within the U.S.)
(212) 647-7706 (outside the U.S.)
(212) 647-7707 FAX

Or browse online by series at www.peterlang.com.